Twenty-First-Century Jim Crow Schools

Twenty-First-Century Jim Crow SCHOOLS

THE IMPACT OF CHARTERS ON PUBLIC EDUCATION

RAYNARD SANDERS,
DAVID STOVALL, and
TERRENDA WHITE

With a Foreword by **KAREN LEWIS**

BEACON PRESS
BOSTON

BEACON PRESS
Boston, Massachusetts
www.beacon.org

Beacon Press books
are published under the auspices of
the Unitarian Universalist Association of Congregations.

21 20 19 18   8 7 6 5 4 3 2 1

This book is printed on acid-free paper that meets the uncoated paper
ANSI/NISO specifications for permanence as revised in 1992.

Text design and composition by Kim Arney

"From Community Schools to Charter Chains: New York's Unequal
Educational Landscape,'" by Terrenda White, was adapted from "Culture,
Power, & Pedagogy(s) in Market-Driven Times: Embedded Case Studies
of Instructional Approaches Across Four Charter Schools in
Harlem, NY," PhD diss., Columbia University, 2014.

Library of Congress Cataloging-in-Publication Data

Names: White, Terrenda, author. | Stovall, David, author. |
Sanders, Raynard, author.
Title: Twenty-first-century Jim Crow schools : the impact of charters
on public education / Terrenda White, David Stovall, and
Raynard Sanders ; with a foreword by Karen Lewis.
Description: Boston : Beacon Press, [2017] | Includes bibliographical references.
Identifiers: LCCN 2017016604 (print) | LCCN 2017030550 (ebook) |
ISBN 9780807076071 (e-book) | ISBN 9780807076064 (pbk. : acid-free paper)
Subjects: LCSH: Charter schools—United States—Case studies. | Charter
schools—Social aspects—United States. | Charter schools—United States—
Finance. | Privatization in education—United States. | Discrimination
in education—United States. | Public schools—United States.
Classification: LCC LB2806.36 (ebook) | LCC LB2806.36 .W543 2017 (print) |
DDC 371.010973—dc23
LC record available at https://lccn.loc.gov/2017016604

Contents

Foreword

Karen Lewis

Raynard Sanders, David Stovall, and Terrenda White have organized excellent, cogent arguments against the corporatization of the charter school movement, which started as a way to have community- and teacher-led schools that served the needs of poor black and brown children.

The writers have demonstrated that the original intent has been usurped by a greedy, oligarchical class intent on tapping into the $600 billion in taxpayer money meant for public schools that has been out of reach for years. The neoliberal education "reform" agenda has been well documented by dozens of scholars, but the charter school industry is finally coming under intense scrutiny as the for-profit sector has gained momentum.

Donald Trump's secretary of education, heiress Betsy DeVos, will likely advocate for the complete eradication of publicly funded, public education while promoting charter chains and vouchers that will exclude the children who are most "difficult" to educate—the English language learners, the disabled, the children who need special services, and the disengaged learners. Sanders et al. have provided an explanation of why market-based "choice" isn't choice at all, but rather an opportunity for the wealthy, the charlatans, the religious warriors, etc., to take advantage of, and reap the spoils from, a devastating economic war of communities that were "left behind" due to the Recession of 2008.

Along the way, Sanders turns his gaze to New Orleans, Stovall takes a hard look at Chicago, and White gives us her perspective on New York. What is particularly interesting is that all three authors tend to recognize the "promise" of charter schools' original intent—providing a high quality education for students whose needs weren't being met in district-run schools with burdensome mandates and inflexible work rules. What the charter operators did was utilize the lack of district oversight and promise better "results" that would cost substantially less because they could have a nonunion workforce.

Unfortunately, it was the beginning of an elaborate hoax. The mom-and pop charters in New York and Chicago were successful at providing nurturing, teacher-led and community-responsive education. Unfortunately, the for-profit chains— operated by former district teachers, Teach for America alumni, and market-driven entrepreneurs—resembled prisons more than the promised innovative new schools. Many of these schools are intent on destroying community "culture," calling it dysfunctional and replacing it with "grit." According to these schools, students need to learn compliance and strict adherence to rules, or they face return to their miserable "failing schools." The elusive results for the profit sector are *test scores*. But for-profit schools refuse to acknowledge that scores tell us much more about family income than what students actually know.

To achieve those scores, several drastic measures had to be taken. It was necessary to develop application criteria that would discourage most—if not all—parents who needed help to navigate the admission process; create marketing plans that used misleading data and false promises (such as a 100 percent graduation rate); establish a mechanism to "cream" the best test scores from neighborhood schools; impose zero-tolerance disciplinary practices for minor offenses, and monetary fines for said offenses; counsel out undesirables (low-scoring students, those with behavior problems); and complain to state and local funding agencies that the charters weren't getting the monies they needed.

These are just a few ways in which the charters cheat the system and the students. In addition, White et al. carefully point out the purposeful starvation of district schools. The reality of charter schools is that some are good and do provide parents with a facsimile of choice, but it is mainly illusory. Stovall says, "Corporate charter schools are positioned as the viable alternative of choice for black and Latinx families that have been 'failed' by the system." He goes on: "Missing from prevailing perceptions of charter schools . . . are the realities of white supremacy, neoliberalism, disinvestment, mass displacement, hypersegregation, and the politics of disposability."

Stovall tells us that the corporate charters provide "false narratives of success . . . while continuing to exclude a significant portion of black and Latinx families" that choose to engage charters.

One of the most pervasive myths (though finally debunked, forcing marketing departments to change their literature) was the 100 percent graduation rate. It didn't seem to matter that only 35 to 65 percent of students who began at the charter school made it to their senior year. This was particularly true for the highly praised Urban Prep Academies, where young black males wear jackets and ties and exude a palpable sense of pride. It took a while for the real story to emerge—that the schools lost about 60 percent of the freshman class. When the reality was exposed, the narrative changed to 100 percent college acceptance rates. Still magnificent, but most people still believe the 100 percent graduation rate because the lie went unchallenged for years. Who would want to burst the bubble of success for young black men in a city so violence prone?

Fear of backlash kept many critics silenced for years. It wasn't until victims of intimidation and harassment came forward that the ugly truth emerged. Another corporate charter chain, which had parlayed its position with the donor class—naming schools after its benefactors—was discovered to have forced students to pay fines of approximately $200,000 per year for minor infractions, such as not wearing belts, and forcing students to repeat entire years for failing a single class, unless they transferred back to their neighborhood schools—this included changing students' transcripts (As miraculously turning into Fs) unless a student agreed to transfer. These are some examples of the unscrupulous depths to which many for-profit corporate charters sink to preserve their claims of success. Stovall likens these practices to the nineteenth-century bait-and-switch promise to freed slaves, of "forty acres and a mule," which turned into debt peonage or the sharecropping system. You are promised a high-quality education, and you get a low-quality, test-and-punish education.

What all authors in this book attempt is to provide the reader with the landscape and history of charter school movements in their respective cities. What is important for us to remember, to contemplate, and to provide a continual analysis of is the fact that the idea of the charter school started innocuously enough, as a way for parents to provide children who needed extra help a way to get it. What we got was something completely different. We must be ever vigilant about the false promises, the marketing tricks, and the bait-and-switch practices of the corporate charter schools that play on the fears and genuine concerns of parents who have the best intentions for their children.

Think about what it takes to label a school, or a child, a "fail-ure." It speaks volumes about what and who is valued in our so-ciety. It says, "We can't fix poverty, so stop using it as an excuse." These are harsh indictments of a system that was designed by the industrialists of the nineteenth century, and an interesting commentary on the robber barons of the twenty-first century, who see profit in an area that should support the broadening of our democratic ideals.

And it is notable that in New Orleans, Chicago, and New York there are no elected boards of education for charter schools. Local control of these systems has been hijacked by business elites in order to create a school system that serves their needs for compliant, noncritical employees. These same elites decry the lack of critical-thinking skills exhibited by to-day's youth as they simultaneously promote for-profit charters that envision a world in which minority children "know their place." That place is often at the back of the line for higher ed-ucation and the concomitant well-paying jobs that hopefully ensue. Those same elites want to hire foreign STEM (science, technology, engineering, and mathematics) workers through the H1-B visa process.

What is missing from this equation is the fact that there are a significant number of older STEM workers who lost their jobs during the Great Recession of 2007–8, as well as a group of young people who got worthless degrees from for-profit col-leges, who have not been able to find work. The chain charter schools have morphed into the K–12 version of that nightmare. While their students may be able to SLANT ("Sit up, Lean for-ward, Ask and answer questions, Nod and Track the teacher") because of the consequences, they have deficits in other areas that arrest their critical-thinking skills. The ability to analyze one's environment can be a student's entrée to a more rigorous educational context, but unfortunately, there are very few jobs that require the skill of bubbling in ovals on an answer sheet.

We are now faced with either a problem, which can be solved, or a dilemma, which must be managed. After reading this book, I hope that real conversations start happening, not only in New Orleans, Chicago, and New York but across the entire country. Are we ready to revert to *Plessy v. Ferguson* days, with a two-tiered system, deeply segregated by race and class across our country, especially in urban areas? Can we have courageous conversations that address the quality of courses and the course offerings that attract students to schools no matter where they're located? Can we have deep, culturally rich curricula that provide all students with the opportunity to have exposure across the spectrum of learning, or will we aspire to STEM job-training courses, which seem to be the focus "du jour" and which will quickly become outdated if we don't prepare our students to analyze data and trends? Where do we want our schools to go, and how do we prepare our students for their futures? Many of the charter proponents have touted choice as the way out of dysfunctional neighborhoods. How is that a real choice? It requires individual families to make individual decisions, yet these so-called dysfunctional neighborhoods have rich traditions and value often overlooked by the elites who control educational opportunities for poor communities of color.

Those of us who work in communities with increasing numbers of charter schools experience the intentional destabilization, the increase in frustration, and the absence of clear policy to help students and the adults who work and care for them grow to their fullest potential. We see how public officials who plan to close schools deliberately starve them first. The chief administrative officer of Chicago Public Schools said in an open bargaining session and in a board of education meeting that if officials knew they were going to close a school in five to ten years, they would put no resources into that school. So how do they know which schools? It's very easy to use and misuse demographic information. What we have found in Chicago is that most schools chosen for the starvation process are by and large those with the largest percentage of longitudinally poor black and/or brown students, in the most segregated communities in the city.

The fight for publicly funded public education is a constant struggle for poor, working-class, and even middle-class families. The introduction of so-called choice and competition in the form of charters is surrounded by opportunity for the ruling class to basically extort monies from already financially strapped public schools, while shifting those funds into the hands of those who benefit the most from the opportunity gap and their friends and families. The pretense of a "better" education is always couched in dubious terms and false or misleading data. Graduation rates have been commingled with college acceptance rates; grade-point averages have been inflated or deflated, depending on a student's desirability; freshman on-track data have been grossly inflated through the huge paperwork burdens imposed on staff members to fail students. The gaming of the statistical system also leads to a significant loss of transparency and community control.

The loss of community control has led to the narrowing of curriculum. Charters are notorious for their emphasis on tested subject areas—mainly reading and math. The loss of social studies—civics and history—has led to a significant decrease in critical thinking and problem solving. Charters are rarely community schools. Children have to be able to leave their neighborhoods, which means parents have to find a way to provide transportation—which leads to creaming. Charters spend a large portion of their budgets on marketing schemes. Many of the charters that have large philanthropy-augmented budgets promised laptops and hundred-dollar signing and/or referral bonuses to cash-strapped families. Several charters in Ohio have been cited for insider dealing. While Ohio is not a subject of this book, the warning signs are clear: without community or public oversight, the incestuous nature of management organizations and their boards can lead to self-dealing and corruption.

If one wants to know how public dollars are spent to enrich private purses, one must *cherchez l'argent*, or, as Deep Throat told Woodward and Bernstein—and as Raynard Sanders suggests here—"Follow the money!" Some of the same bad actors pop up in Florida, Connecticut, and Louisiana. One such debacle brought about the fall of a Latinx rising star, Juan Rangel, mentioned in David Stovall's essay on Chicago. Rangel received a $92 million investment from the state of Illinois to fund his charter schools. The board of his community organization and the board of the charter school network were essentially the same. Lucrative construction contracts that didn't pass ethical muster were given to relatives of board members. The only way to pay off bondholders was to expand, whether communities wanted the schools or not. The giant Ponzi scheme fell through. The way to keep the schools financially stable was to pay teachers and staff poorly. They frequently employed zealous Teach for America corps members and at-will employees, while administrators commanded middle-six-figure salaries. As a matter of fact, Rangel made more money as an administrator of thirteen schools than did the CEO of Chicago Public Schools, who oversaw more than 550 schools.

The inherent flaws in charter schools are beautifully captured by our three authors, who have worked to provide you with food for thought on models of choice. Charters give us a clear plan for providing a substandard education, even as they try to convince the public that they're bringing a quality product. What makes it all the more satisfying is that each of the authors in their way demonstrates the true meaning of "bait and switch." It is a shame that so much funding that could have been used to adequately and equitably run public schools is given to those who couldn't care less about the children who not only need, but indeed deserve, an excellent education.

The New Orleans Public Education Experiment

CHILDREN LOSE—EDUCATION REFORMERS WIN

Raynard Sanders

M ore than twelve years after Hurricane Katrina, New Orleans finds itself in the belly of the beast. The movement to privatize public education in America, with the support of the federal government and several opportunistic members of the philanthropic community, has taken strong root here. Due to the machinations of this "private-public" partnership, New Orleans has the largest percentage of charter schools of any city in the country, and it has become the darling of the growing education industry.

The local public school district, under the Orleans Parish School Board (OPSB), manages six traditional public schools and twenty-two charter schools, while the Louisiana Department of Education manages sixty-nine publicly funded private charter schools. The phrase "publicly funded private schools"— an oxymoron if there ever was one—perfectly epitomizes charter schools in New Orleans, which operate with unquestioned authority, without accountability to individual school communities or the public.

The education reforms implemented after Hurricane Katrina were more about changes in local governance than anything else, as the new model reestablished New Orleans's "politically incorrect" tiered school system, which had offered drastically different education services to students based on race and class. In many ways, the New Orleans model circumvents the *Brown v. Board of Education* case of 1954, which struck down the separate but equal doctrine rendered in the *Plessy v. Ferguson* case of 1896. Today, public education in New Orleans is directed by a cadre of white people, with no input from a largely African American population. In the last decade, the public schools in New Orleans have, by and large, become profit centers for a few charter operators with no interest, expertise, or desire to improve academic achievement.

In selling this scheme, the education reformers developed a well-financed narrative that touts unprecedented academic success, in which the charter schools are not only outperforming the public schools in Louisiana but in some areas are outperforming public schools across the country. The irresistible narrative about "charter school miracles" in New Orleans has spread across the country like wildfire. The story has all the bells and whistles of a Hollywood movie—a public school system made up of mostly poor and minority students suffering from years of academic failure, ruled by corrupt school board members and staff, with lazy teachers. In the end, the kids are saved by a knight in shining white armor. In selling this scheme, education reformers present a well-financed narrative touting academic success, boasting of charter schools that outperform public schools in Louisiana and across the country. However, the real story is that education reforms in New Orleans have been a dismal failure academically and operationally. To make matters worse, the reforms have reactivated equity and access crises that were resolved in the courts decades ago. Finally, schools in New Orleans have been turned into profit centers for untrained and inexperienced white entrepreneurs who, in many ways, play the roles of plantation owners.

Shortly after Hurricane Katrina devastated New Orleans, local and state education officials were given full free range by federal officials to create an all-charter school district. They were given everything that economist Milton Friedman and others had been promoting for years to improve America's failing public education system—public schools run by the private sector without government oversight, with no duly elected school board, and no teachers' union contracts, having fired all those old tired teachers who were responsible for failing schools. The first step was taken by then governor Kathleen Blanco in October 2005—just one month after the hurricane—when she issued an executive order removing parent and faculty participation in starting charter schools. Thirty days later, the Louisiana legislature passed an illegal and unconstitutional policy that took the governance of public schools from the locally elected school board and gave it to Louisiana Department of Education officials. In short order, state education officials turned the governance of public schools to unelected private charter school boards, which were unaccountable to the parents and the community.

The charter model was then sold to parents and children in New Orleans, the schools presented as inclusive entities where all children mattered. Unfortunately, these education reforms amount to the same exclusive system, in which quality services are provided to a targeted group of students who are white, affluent, and academically talented. Black and brown families and children have, once again, been left out in this new equation, and those in most severe need are least likely to receive quality education.

A BRIEF HISTORY OF PUBLIC EDUCATION IN NEW ORLEANS

Education was not a priority in Louisiana, which was one of several states that did not offer education services to slaves. In 1830, Louisiana, like many other Southern states, passed anti-literacy laws, because, it was commonly believed, literacy tended to excite dissatisfaction and produce insurrectionist attitudes in the minds of slaves.[1] Public education in New Orleans officially began in 1841, led by former minister and New England educator John Shaw, recommended to city officials by Horace Mann, considered the father of the common school in Boston and the national education expert of his day. Shaw patterned schools in New Orleans after Boston schools, including grammar schools and high schools. At that time, the common school was a new concept in which Mann saw education as the equalizer for poverty and sought to make education available to all, not restricted to students by class. Shaw saw fit to mention his position on teaching slaves to Mann, who opposed slavery but avoided the issue in developing public schools. He wrote:

> I cannot say I have no objection to slavery, but having formerly owned and been myself a slaveholder in Mississippi, I am too well acquainted with the state of slavery of things in that part of the world . . . [t]o have any wish to interfere with the institutions or disturb the tranquility of the south.[2]

There was considerable disagreement among policymakers about the role of public education in Louisiana. As in many Southern states, where the major industry was agriculture supported by the free labor of slaves, in Louisiana there was no strong consensus that public education was needed or important.[3] The Louisiana legislature provided less than minimal funding, and as a result school districts across the state had to fight even to stay open, much less provide quality educational services. New Orleans was the only city in the state that made significant progress in developing a public education system. From 1862—when New Orleans was seized by the Union army and placed under the control of General Benjamin F. Butler—until 1877, free public education was offered to all, including slaves living in the city. This arrangement ended with the contested presidential election of 1876. An agreement, the Compromise of 1877, was struck between Republicans and Democrats that returned control of the former Confederacy back to the states and, in the process, ensured Rutherford B. Hayes's election as president.[4] This in essence ended Reconstruction and all the gains toward including former slaves in the governmental process. The Compromise of 1877 led to the appointment of a new school board in New Orleans and ended integration in the city's public schools. The new leaders who took over state government never had any interests in public education, and thus began the deterioration of public education in New Orleans. The accomplishments achieved during Reconstruction quickly disappeared. The state legislature cut the funding for schools drastically, reducing the $5 million school tax to $1 million. The New Orleans public school superintendent noted that funding for schools fell below the level of funding in the 1850s.[5]

In 1891, a diverse group of community leaders in New Orleans, calling itself the Comité des Citoyens (Committee of Citizens), came together to plan a challenge to a new Louisiana law, the Separate Car Act of 1890. Presented as an "act to promote comfort of passengers in railway trains," the law forced railway companies to provide separate coaches for black and white passengers. While this law pleased segregationists, it forced railroads to provide an extra car for African Americans, even if only five purchased tickets. After months of planning and raising money, the Comité des Citoyens chose Homer Plessy to stage a protest on board. On June 7, 1892, Plessy was arrested at the corner of Press and Royal Streets in New Orleans for violating the law. On November 18, 1892, Judge John Howard Ferguson ruled against Plessy, and the Louisiana Supreme Court upheld his decision. Later, in 1895, Ferguson's decision was appealed to the United States Supreme Court as the landmark *Plessy v. Ferguson* case. When the court upheld the previous rulings, on May 18, 1896, the separate but equal doctrine became the established law of the land, and for fifty-eight years served as the legal basis for maintaining segregation in public schools across the country. In New Orleans, schools remained segregated until six years after the US Supreme Court ruled in 1954 that the separate but equal doctrine was unconstitutional and ordered the integration of public schools in America.[6]

Though "separate but equal" was ostensibly the law, it was not enforced in New Orleans. By 1900, the city's public schools offered inferior educational services and facilities at its few black schools compared to services offered at white schools. Education for African Americans was not a priority for the school board and its leadership. In 1902, in a report to the OPSB from Assistant Superintendent Nicholas Bauer to Superintendent Warren Easton, Bauer clearly explains New Orleans's sentiment regarding the education of black students: "To teach the negro is a different problem. His natural ability is that of low character and it is possible to bring him to a certain level beyond which is impossible to carry him. That point is the fifth grade of our schools."[7]

Over the years, the OPSB has provided three times more funding for white students than for black students, with white students also receiving more educational options in an array of new school buildings for most of the twentieth century. Even after the *Brown v. Board of Education* decision in 1954, the school district selectively built new school facilities in communities with largely white student populations. Black students were left to languish in inadequate facilities, often in older buildings previously used by white students.

As desegregation efforts were under way across the country following *Brown*, laws were passed by the Louisiana legislature in 1960 to take control of public schools in New Orleans away from OPSB in an effort to avoid an order from a federal judge to desegregate the schools. A federal judge overruled the state legislature and ordered the OPSB local to comply with the desegregation order. Since then, there have been other attempts by local businesses and their political allies to dismantle or take over the school district.

As the numbers of African American students in the district grew, the white business community and civic leaders gradually pulled financial support. They refused to back numerous efforts by the school board to pass taxes for improvements, such as renovating and replacing the district's aging school buildings; increasing per pupil expenditures; and installing air conditioning in schools. This lack of community support resulted in a backlog of more than a billion dollars in needed improvements by the time of Hurricane Katrina.

In the early 1990s, some political leaders proposed dividing the district into two because, as I recall, the district was considered too large and too bureaucratic for the city to effectively address its myriad challenges. This recommendation essentially would have created one school district of mostly minority and poor students and another district, made up of Uptown schools, attended mostly by white students, in an area where most magnet schools were situated. The public rejected this proposal, as it was clear it would have merely deepened the separation by race and class.

In the late 1990s, Louisiana adopted a new school account-ability system measuring student success and school quality solely by standardized tests, in keeping with a national trend. The state instituted high-stakes testing in the fourth and eighth grades, and began to use student test performance to determine promotion. The high schools had been using a graduate exit exam since 1991. Under the new system, schools serving large poor-student populations struggled and received low rankings. More than 85 percent of the student population of New Orleans, the largest district in the state, was below the poverty level, and a large number of the city's schools did not meeting the new state standards. However, over the decade, many public schools in New Orleans began to improve, with most of them meeting their annual growth plan as determined by the state department of education.

HURRICANE KATRINA: A GAME CHANGER

The New Orleans public school system before Hurricane Katrina resembled typical urban school systems across the country. Educators struggled to provide good learning environments for many poor and minority students with limited resources. The public school district operated a small cadre of schools (most of which had admission requirements) that provided a quality learning environment; this was where the system's white students studied. While most schools providing for middle-class and poor students struggled to provide quality learning environments, many of these schools offered students a great learning environment considering the challenges. Consequently, New Orleans had some of highest- and lowest-performing schools in the state of Louisiana.

Pre-Katrina New Orleans schools clearly had problems academically but were improving, with 80 percent of schools meeting their annual academic goals. However, New Orleans had some systemic problems that plagued every urban school district in the country. Right after Katrina, as students slowly returned to the city and an abundance of funds flowed from the philanthropic community and unnamed foreign countries, New Orleans had the opportunity of a lifetime to create optimal learning environments for all kids in its public schools, and might have well addressed the systemic problems that inhibited academic achievement by children with the greatest need.

Hurricane Katrina formed over the Bahamas on August 23, 2005, and hit the Mississippi Gulf Coast on the morning of August 29. Most public schools in the region were either destroyed or severely damaged, yet there were several schools that received little or no damage. Its maintenance facilities and transportation center were under water, as were hundreds of school buses. The school board administrative offices located on the west bank of the Mississippi River received extensive wind damage, and broken windows and leaking roofs led to water damage.

As most of the country struggled to understand the loss of life and damage, the lack of government response to Katrina in New Orleans led many to conclude that federal officials were inexcusably asleep at the wheel. However, some began to perceive a more nefarious plan—that the city presented a golden opportunity for the private sector to establish a new model of governance. Clues appeared within days of Katrina, in articles featuring quotes from Uptown residents (who lived in the city's wealthiest community). James Reiss, chairman of the New Orleans Regional Transit Authority, the board that oversaw public transportation, was in contact with about forty New

Orleans business leaders after the storm. They met with the mayor and insisted the remade New Orleans would not simply restore the old order in a city they considered burdened by poor people. "Those who want to see this city rebuilt want to see it done in a completely different way: demographically, geographically, and politically," Reiss said. "I'm not just speaking for myself here."[8]

As the federal government bungled its response to Katrina, conservative education groups and the "education industry" in Washington and Baton Rouge were ready to pounce with a unified message: this was an "opportunity" to create a new paradigm of publicly funded, market-based schools that provided "flexibility" for individual families.[9] Even before Katrina floodwaters had subsided, the *Wall Street Journal*'s Brendan Miniter wrote a column, on September 6, 2005, headlined "A Silver Lining?" Miniter wrote that Katrina "presents New Orleans officials with an opportunity . . . for rebuilding New Orleans's school system." Miniter urged officials to downplay teacher "certification requirements" and promote charter schools.[10]

On September 7, 2005, the Heritage Foundation released a memorandum on Gulf Coast recovery urging Congress to suspend a law requiring federal contractors to pay their workers the prevailing wage, to repeal or waive portions of the Clean Air Act, to eliminate or postpone various taxes, and to promote "new educational options," including "charter schools, as well as private and religious schools."[11] President George W. Bush used these recommendations as the framework for rebuilding New Orleans after Katrina. The recommendations were released even as bodies were still floating in putrid water. It was clear that powerful national forces had plans to privatize public schools in New Orleans, turning them over to "deserving" entrepreneurs.

Leigh Dingerson was familiar with the public school land-scape in New Orleans from working with the Student at the Center writing program at Frederick Douglass High School in 2004. Shortly after Hurricane Katrina, Dingerson began to follow online discussions about rebuilding the New Orleans public school system. She noticed that many groups and individuals who were anti–public education were leading the discussion. Discussion leaders included many members of the Education Industry Association—a trade organization representing corporations that market services to schools and school districts. Others were from conservative think tanks such as the Center for Education Reform, the Thomas B. Fordham Foundation, the Heritage Foundation, and the University of Washington's Center for Reinventing Education.[12]

Paul Hill, founder of the Center on Reinventing Public Education, further advanced private sector interests in an Urban Institute report he coauthored, *The Future of Public Education in New Orleans*, which stated that "education could be one of the bright spots in New Orleans' recovery effort, which may even establish a new model for school districts nationally." Hill and coauthor Jane Hannaway advocated refusing to rebuild the New Orleans public schools, firing the teachers (and by extension dissolving the teachers' union), eradicating the central administration, and inviting for-profit corporations (with sordid histories), such as the Edison Schools and other organizations, to take over running schools. New Orleans had suddenly become the perfect city for school profiteers to finally make their dream come true.[13]

Machinations began at the local level, with Cecil Picard, Louisiana schools superintendent at the time, playing a central role. On September 14, 2005, Picard sent a letter to the US Department of Education requesting $2.4 billion to pay out-of-work employees (teachers and staff) of school districts impacted by the hurricane. Picard requested more than $622 million for salaries and $155 million for benefits.[14] It was later discovered that, after the federal funds were received, state education officials provided payroll assistance to other school districts affected by Hurricane Katrina and withheld funds from employees of OPSB. (Employees from New Orleans received pay only for days they worked before Hurricane Katrina.) State education officials gave funds to the Recovery School District, which used them to recruit untrained, out-of-state teachers (mostly from Teach for America) to replace certified and trained teachers of Orleans Parish.

Just weeks after Katrina, the federal government began to direct funding for the rebuilding of public schools in New Orleans. Secretary of Education Margaret Spellings announced a Department of Education grant of $20.9 million for the establishment of charter schools in Louisiana.[15] It was the federal government's first move to destroy public education in New Orleans, and a step that was in accord with the Heritage Foundation agenda announced a few weeks earlier. On October 7, 2005, just five weeks after Katrina, Governor Blanco had issued the executive order waiving the Louisiana Department of Education's charter school requirements, thus allowing anyone to open charter schools.[16] The order essentially allowed charter schools to open overnight, without local district parent or faculty input, knowledge, or approval. Until that time, there had been a process in place for public schools to become charter schools, it required a vote of approval from faculty and parents. Blanco's order was, by far, the most devastating blow to the city of New Orleans, where more than 1,800 citizens had died or lost their homes and possessions in the flood waters a few weeks earlier. Within weeks after the devastation, while citizens were still struggling to find love ones, Governor Blanco was removing their input in the public education process, a right afforded to every other citizen in Louisiana.

And as other school districts affected by Hurricane Katrina were making plans to reopen, Superintendent Picard withheld funds from the OPSB, saying initially that the district's schools were not ready to reopen, and later indicating that the schools would not be ready until the 2006–2007 school year. It should be noted that New Orleans wasn't completely underwater; there were numerous neighborhoods, including the entire west bank of the Mississippi River, that did not flood. Hundreds of families began returning to the city within weeks of Katrina, looking to put their kids back in school. Darryl Kilbert, then deputy superintendent of Orleans Parish schools, said state education officials came up with one excuse after another for why they were not releasing funds to reopen the city's schools. One excuse was that the city and schools had suffered extensive damages. Yet funds had been released to neighboring school districts, including St. Bernard and Plaquemines public schools, which had suffered more damage than New Orleans. (Plaquemines public schools had been completely destroyed.)

Picard and his supporters attempted to wrest control away from the OPSB. On November 30, 2005, in a special session at the request of Picard and with the support of Governor Blanco, the Louisiana legislature passed Act 35, which illegally took practically all public schools in New Orleans away from the OPSB and put them under the authority of the Recovery School District (RSD), a state-run district for failing schools. In addition to authorizing and overseeing charter schools, the RSD became an operator of regular directly run schools. It gained authority over 112 of the 128 public schools in New Orleans. Many of the 112 buildings were believed to be beyond repair or were no longer in operation. Act 35 changed the criteria by which schools were labeled failing, and it expanded the RSD's takeover authority. The legislation applied only to public schools in New Orleans; it was clearly discriminatory.

In Louisiana, a public school is determined to be "academically unacceptable" (AU) based on its school performance score (SPS), a composite based on one of three student performance exams, the school's dropout rate, and its student attendance rate. Before Act 35, a public school was labeled AU if it didn't achieve a score of 60 for the 2004–2005 school year. A school designated AU for four consecutive years would be classified as "failing," a status that makes the schools eligible for state takeover via the RSD. Before Act 35, a "failing" school was moved into the RSD only if a chartering organization formally requested to assume management of the school. Act 35 changed the rules significantly, allowing the state to take control of schools with SPS scores below the state average (87.4 in 2004–2005), even if the schools had not been AU for four straight years. Act 35 expanded the state's takeover authority so that it, in effect, applied only to New Orleans and one other school district in the state.

Shortly after Hurricane Katrina, on September 13, 2005, Superintendent Picard wrote education secretary Spellings a letter requesting $2 billion to help restart the schools in the parishes affected by Hurricanes Katrina and Rita. He stated that some of the funds would be used to keep the teachers on the payroll and to maintain their health insurance. Picard referenced a similar situation in Florida after a hurricane; the federal government had given Florida $100 million to pay teachers, who worked assisting Federal Emergency Management Agency (FEMA) officials with recovery until the schools reopened.

Picard received $622 million for salaries and $135 million for benefits for out-of-work school employees from the federal government.[17] While other parishes affected by Hurricane Katrina received emergency pay for teachers and staff, the funds allocated for New Orleans were directed to the RSD and used to recruit teachers nationally for New Orleans and the Gulf region.

In December 2005, with few schools and little money under its control, OPSB passed a resolution firing 7,500 school employees who had been on "disaster leave without pay," an employment status that did not exist in school board policy.[18] OPSB claimed it dismissed the teachers because the district did not have any schools or funds after Act 35. It did not have anywhere for the employees to work because the state-run RSD controlled nearly all New Orleans schools, as well as most of the board's operating budget—approximately 7,500 employees, including teachers, administrators, support personnel, maintenance workers, bus drivers, and custodians—all let go illegally contrary to local and state policy. The RSD claimed that after taking over most of public schools in New Orleans, it was not obligated to hire them, despite state tenure laws. (It should be noted, when the state reopened schools in March 2006, it refused to honor teacher tenure laws of the teachers from OPSB and required all teacher applicants to take a test.) Most of the 7,500 employees were African Americans with livable-wage jobs, and their dismissal was a serious blow to the African American middle class in New Orleans.

Even more devastating was the absence of an outcry from political and civic leadership. After being almost destroyed by one of the greatest natural and manmade disasters in the history of this country, a poor city lost 7,500 livable-wage jobs—and the leadership didn't stand up and demand that residents keep their jobs. Instead, most of the city's leadership applauded the move and welcomed the change.

The fired employees of New Orleans filed a lawsuit. Judge Ethel Julien, in 2012, found that a special policy for force reductions at a time of economic crisis requires the creation of a "recall list," designed to fill vacancies with those who had been laid off, and that even in that situation, employees who had been dismissed were entitled to hearings. Judge Julien found that none of the local and state policies were followed, and ruled in favor of the teachers. The state appealed the case to the Louisiana Supreme Court, which unexpectedly overturned Judge Julien's decision.[19] After this disappointing loss, the attorneys appealed the case to the US Supreme Court on the grounds that the fired employees' due process rights were violated under the Fourteenth Amendment. Unfortunately, the Court refused to hear the case.[20]

CHARTER SCHOOLS HAVE FAILED ACADEMICALLY

After seizing public schools in New Orleans before opening any schools, state officials were predicting academic success. In November 2005, Governor Blanco declared that a state takeover would create a "new birth of excellence and opportunity" for the city's schoolchildren. A document by state officials promoting the takeover plan identified the mission of the RSD as the creation of a "world-class" school system in which "every decision focuses on the best interests of the children."[21]

Yet, education reformers' claims of success in New Orleans have been dismissed by practically all external sources. Below are analyses done ten years after Hurricane Katrina, in 2015, by longtime researcher Michael Deshotels. He compared RSD

charter schools with other Louisiana school districts and concluded the following:

- 83 percent of Louisiana public schools outperform RSD
  schools in math and English language.[22]
- 94 percent of schools in public systems produce better
  ACT results than do schools in the RSD.
- The RSD is near the bottom, among seventy Louisiana
  systems, in percentage of students graduating.
- The RSD has the highest percentage of students leaving
  school before ninth grade.
- Even though most RSD schools are advertised as college
  prep, only 5.5 percent of RSD students taking Advanced
  Placement courses passed the credit exams.
- Most Louisiana public schools, including those in the
  RSD, have improved state scores in the ten years since
  Katrina, but the state's comparative ranking with other
  states has declined.
- Louisiana has produced significant test-grade inflation
  by lowering raw cut scores on state tests. Real achieve-
  ment is only slightly improved as measured by the
  NAEP test.

Additionally, Deshotels states that several times Louisiana
has changed the criteria for passing a failing school, which has
resulted in lower standards since 2005. Calculation methods for
school and district performance scores have changed over the
ten years since the school takeover. Cut scores for state tests
have changed since the takeover, and in the last three years, the
underlying cut scores for grade level performance have been re-
duced significantly. School grade inflation may have produced
"faux" progress in nearly all Louisiana schools.[23]

In a policy brief, Dr. Julian Vasquez Heilig of California State University Sacramento addressed New Orleans's claims of success in key educational indicators, including the claim that the RSD dropout rates and high graduation rate was highest in Louisiana, at 61.1 percent. Heilig concluded that the RSD is still the biggest dropout and "push out" factory in the state, with many low-performing students leaving school as early as the seventh and eighth grades. He also concluded that national comparative data suggest there is a dearth of evidence supporting a decade of test-score-driven, state-takeover, charter-conversion model education, as implemented in New Orleans. A preponderance of data suggests that the top-down, privately controlled "education reforms" imposed on New Orleans have failed. The state and the RSD place last and nearly last in rankings based on national and federal data. These results do not deserve accolades.[24]

In These Times reported on research conducted for the Network for Public Education by University of Arizona researchers Francesca López and Amy Olson that compared charters, mostly in New Orleans, with other Louisiana public schools, controlling for factors including race, ethnicity, and poverty, and whether students qualified for special education. On eighth-grade reading and math tests, charter school students performed significantly worse than did their noncharter public school counterparts. The researchers also found the gap between charter and noncharter public school performance in Louisiana to be the largest of any state in the country. Louisiana's overall scores were the fourth-lowest in the nation.[25]

It should be noted that after raising the SPS for state takeover of schools in 2005, the state has lowered the score, thus changing the criteria for labeling schools as failing—a clear indication of how the Louisiana Department of Education labels schools for political reasons.

State and local officials have a serious problem validating claims of low dropout rates and high graduation rates, because the RSD does not have a centralized enrollment system. The *New York Times* ran an opinion piece by Andrea Gabor, who said:

> One problem is that in the decentralized charter system, no agency is responsible for keeping track of all kids. Two years ago, the Recovery School District, acknowledging that it was "worried" about high school attrition, began assigning counselors to help relocate students from schools it was closing. Louisiana's official dropout rates are unreliable, but a new report by Measure of America, a project of the Social Science Research Council, using Census Bureau survey data from 2013, found that over 26,000 people in the metropolitan area between the ages of 16 and 24 are counted as "disconnected," because they are neither working nor in school.[26]

The New Orleans *Times-Picayune* newspaper also reported the problem with the accuracy of student data in making analysis relative to the absence of a centralized enrollment system. For one school year, the RSD didn't have documentation validating that students had transferred to another school or moved abroad. Without properly coded transfers, they reported that "RSD graduation and dropout rates are questionable."[27]

Over the last few years, John White, the current state superintendent of education, has been an assiduous and sometimes untruthful spinner of good stories about Louisiana, especially regarding RSD academic progress. White has controlled much of the accountability environment in the state, but he has a problem with data he can't control—particularly ACT scores. The ACT is a college readiness assessment that students in

Louisiana are required to take. The maximum score a student can earn on the ACT is a 36. A student needs a score of 17 to get into a Louisiana university.

For years White has played games with the release of ACT scores. In 2015 he released partial returns, and he later embargoed ACT scores. Researcher Mercedes Schneider reported that White released one set of RSD ACT scores in July 2015, but when she reviewed the annual school's report card, Schneider noticed that the scores were lower. She noted that "according to 2014–15 school and district report cards, which were released in October 2015, the RSD New Orleans average ACT composite was not the July-advertised 16.6 but instead, 15.6."[28] Schneider stated that RSD ACT scores ranged from a 7.2 to 19.6, with only one of its eleven schools exceeding the 2014–15 state average of 19.2. It should be noted that many of these charter high schools are college preparatory, yet their composite scores are below the admission to a university in Louisiana.

LOW GRADES FOR SCHOOL CHOICE

School reformers claim urban students are failing because the students are stuck in failing neighborhood public schools and don't have access to good schools outside of their communities. They repeatedly claim "that parents can walk with their feet if they are not pleased with their child's school." New Orleans's RSD advertises itself as the national model for school choice, claiming to be the only all choice public school district in the country, however, it has not been good for parents and students. After Hurricane Katrina, each charter school's attendance zone became the entire city, resulting in the elimination of neighborhood schools. In theory, parents had school choice, with the ability to select any school in the city.

Immediately after Hurricane Katrina, each individual charter school began to handle its admissions without any guidelines or oversight from the RSD. Charter schools had their own selection processes, and most of them did not use a lottery, with each school controlling its admission requirements and condition on admission. This process was confusing to parents. One parent who recently moved to New Orleans expressed her frustration in trying to get her children into a charter school with academic admission requirements:

> I got a letter saying that I failed to attend the open house that I didn't know about and therefore the children are not eligible. My fault (through ignorance—I had no idea). It's ironic. I sat through hours of Lusher Charter School meetings. I'm so frustrated by this process that I can hardly stand it. I was advised by a local woman yesterday that I should volunteer at Audubon Charter School to get my kids in. She said that is how her friend got her child enrolled. Everybody has a way-in speech for me. I think I need to get myself a new job and get them in private school. It will cost me a fortune, but at least it will be a reasonable and transparent process.[29]

Needless to say, the individual school registration process was a nightmare. After numerous complaints, in 2012 the RSD implemented the OneApp school registration process in which parents could submit a single application and make several school selections for their child. The RSD said the new One-App computerized lottery system would solve all the problems and make the process much easier for parents. Like other RSD programs, it was a disaster from the beginning. The process was complicated, with parents having to complete a twelve-page registration form. Parents complained about siblings being sent to different schools, and about a lack of consideration for students with special needs. One parent said that she filled out the application and listed three preferred choices but didn't receive any of them. According to the parent when she received her child's assignment she noticed three additional schools added to her three choices, and her child was assigned sixth choice, a failing voucher school.

Researcher Jan Resseger stated that New Orleans has bragged about its new OneApp system and how it has made it easier for students to apply for schools,[30] but the authors of "Whose Choice? Student Experiences and Outcomes in the New Orleans School Marketplace" explain that OneApp has not really increased opportunity for most students:

> A parent's desire to send his or her child to a particular school does not result in the child going there. Admission to that school is predicated on a host of factors that are out of the parent's control, such as the neighborhood, the availability of spots, the lottery number if the student is on a waiting list, and the child's academic and behavioral record or special needs. The desirability of the school available to a family is closely related to the desirability of the child from the perspective of the school, including the likelihood that the child will behave well, work hard, and perform well on state tests that . . . will determine the school's reputation and ongoing survival. [31]

Parents and community members complained that students assembled daily on the streets of New Orleans as early as 5:45 a.m. to catch school buses and returned home after 5 p.m. The students, whose grades ranged from kindergarten to twelfth grade, rode daily to and from school for an hour and a half each day.

In New Orleans, it is not unusual to find five- and six-year-old students who endure twelve-hour days in search of a good education.

CHALLENGES TO EQUITY AND ACCESS

Shortly after the RSD started operating schools in 2006, parents and advocates began to notice problems with charter schools admitting students with special needs and/or serving students with special needs as required by federal law. Some students were completely denied enrollment because of their disability, or were forced to attend schools that lacked resources necessary to serve them. Students with special needs were punished by suspension in record numbers. Meanwhile, other students' disabilities were completely overlooked because they had not been identified. While charter schools had no problem admitting gifted children and providing special-needs services to them, they ignored the needs of children who are on the autism spectrum, developmentally disabled, or who require additional learning services.

After more than five years of trying to get problems they experienced with local RSD and state education officials addressed, a group of parents and advocates led by the Southern Poverty Law Center filed a class action suit against the RSD and the Louisiana Department of Education. The center noted:

> According to state data, the Louisiana Department of Education (LDE) has systemically failed to fulfill these obligations to New Orleans public school students with disabilities. The results are abysmal.
>
> The graduation rate for RSD students with disabilities is less than half of the overall graduation rate.

Only 6.8% of RSD students with disabilities exit with a high school diploma, while across the state, the average is 19.4%.

In the 2008–09 school year, RSD schools suspended nearly 30% of all students with disabilities—a rate that is 63% higher than the state average.

During the 2007–08 school year, 94.6% of eighth grade RSD students with disabilities failed the Louisiana Educational Assessment Program (LEAP) exam. For the same year, 78.3% of all eighth-grade charter school students with disabilities failed the LEAP.

On average, school districts throughout Louisiana have identified 12.2% of their students as eligible for special education services. New Orleans Public Schools have identified only 8% of their students as eligible for special education services. Comparable school districts throughout the country identify almost twice as many students with disabilities.[32]

After five years, the lawsuit was settled before trial in 2015. For the first time in the history of New Orleans public schools, a federal judge issued a consent decree and appointed a special monitor to ensure that children with special needs were being served as required under federal law. While this is disappointing, it is not surprising; despite all of the efforts to improve the system, schools were allowed to discriminate against students with special needs. But given the history of inequity in Louisiana public schools it is not surprising.

OUT-OF-CONTROL CHARTER SCHOOLS

The education reform movement routinely ignores sound research, and it ignores best practices. In New Orleans, students from mostly poor African American communities attend charter schools that use the "no excuses" model that prepares students more for prison than for college. Such practices as harsh disciplinary rules for minor infractions, suspending and expelling students and sending them home without notifying the parents, and the bullying and harassment of special needs students, which, in one case, was encouraged by a teacher; the school refused to listen to parents' complaints. These kinds of practices are inhumane and unethical—no child in America should be exposed to this abuse, especially in school. A *USA Today* article reported abuses at New Orleans College Prep: after breakfast and roll call, reading teacher Anne Felter walked through the aisles and distributed twenty-six large, laminated "YET" signs to selected students—those deemed "not there yet." The signs were given to students who acted up in class or who failed to meet work requirements, Felter said. The students wore the signs around their necks for three days, could not talk to other students, and had to eat lunch alone, she said. The signs were removed only after face-to-face conferences between the students' parents and Ben Kleban, the school's director.[33]

A civil rights complaint filed in 2014 against New Orleans charter school managers Collegiate Academies alleged that discipline is so harsh that it violates federal laws and verges on abuse. One of Collegiate Academies' schools, which have selective admission policies, was cited in 2010 on *The Oprah Winfrey Show* as a model school and received a check for $1 million from the star's Angel Network. Students at G. W. Carver, also a Collegiate Academies school, but which does not have a selective admission policy—have a different experience, in which harsh disciplinary policies are a part of their daily routines. A group calling itself the Better Education Support Team asked the civil rights divisions of the US departments of education and justice to investigate the inhumane discipline policies at Carver. A list of grievances extracted from the complaint:

- *Out of control suspension practices for trivial matters and policies*: From 2012–2013, the three Collegiate Academies schools had the highest out-of-school suspension rates in the city of New Orleans with Carver Prep suspending out-of-school 61.36 percent of its students in one year, Carver Collegiate 68.85 percent, and Sci Academy at 38.9 percent.
- *Isolating students as discipline*: Carver Prep and Carver Collegiate deprive students of their right to an education when they suspend students in-school by "sidelining" them or "benching" them and keeping them in a room by themselves for the entire day or in another teacher's classroom without giving them any work from their classes to do for the day, so that they miss out on their class work because of minor rule violations such as being out of uniform by wearing the wrong type of belt or having jewelry on.
- *Sending students home without notifying parents*: Students report that they are sent home without the school notifying their parents.
- *Detaining students until they have to go home after dark*: Parents and guardians have reported that their child is given after school detention even though the parent has expressed to the school that they are not comfortable with their child taking public transportation home in the dark.
- *Expelling students from the school bus without parental notification*: Students have reported being expelled from riding the school bus and their parent was never informed.

- *Failure to report injuries to parents*: Carver Prep fails to report students' injuries to the child's parents and does not report them to a nurse when requested and needed.
- *Bullying and harassment of children with special needs*: Students with Individualized Education Plans have reported being placed in the back of the classroom repeatedly and denied participation in the class due to their "misbehavior."
- *Lack of legally required notice to parents of children with disabilities*: The Individuals with Disabilities Education Act of 2004 (IDEA) requires that parents and legal guardians of children with disabilities receive notice of any meetings with respect to the identification, evaluation, and educational placement of the child. Carver Collegiate did not inform Student O's mother of the meeting the school held to update the student's Individualized Education Plan (IEP). The school lied about contacting the student's mother and stated in the IEP that the student's "family was called by his advisor to set up an IEP meeting. They were unable to attend." His mother said she never knew about the meeting. Carver Collegiate violated the notice provisions under IDEA and deprived this student's guardian and advocate of her role on the IEP team and her right to inform the team about services her child needed at the school.
- *Illegal suspensions of special needs students for more than ten days*: Students with disabilities at Carver Prep and Carver Collegiate report that they have been suspended more than ten times.
- *Failure to provide parents copies of student handbook*: Carver Collegiate and Carver Prep have violated due process by not giving parents and guardians copies of the

student handbook so that they have notice of what the
rules and procedures are and how they can appeal their
child's suspension.

- *Punitive bathroom policies*: Students report that bathroom doors are locked and they must request permission
to go to the bathroom, which is often not given.

- *Punishment through withholding meals*: Sci Academy
does not provide lunch as a form of punishment against
students who have chosen not to serve lunch detention.
The food students do receive is often spoiled. Students
complain of constantly feeling hungry because they feel
they are not receiving enough food to eat at school and
have been told that they may not bring food from home.

- *Intimidation of students exercising First Amendment
rights*: The Collegiate Academies schools all violate students' freedom of speech rights by retaliating against
them for protesting and suspending students for engaging in out-of-school protests. One student was suspended for "instigating a protest" and prevented from
meeting with school staff to discuss the students' list of
demands because she was suspended. This kind of retaliation against students exercising their right to assembly
creates a culture of fear and intimidation at these schools
causing many students to fear retaliation for challenging
rules and policies they believe to be unfair. Many students have refused to contact advocates for help because
they were afraid the school would retaliate and expel
them for speaking out.[34]

Also in 2014, a national coalition filed a federal civil rights
complaint alleging Louisiana's school closure policies discriminated against black children, asserting that under the state's

policy and practice, African American schools have closed at a much higher and faster rate than schools with greater percentages of white students. A second allegation was that Louisiana discriminated against African American students by keeping them trapped in failing schools.[35]

FREE GOVERNMENT MONEY FOR SCHOOL REFORMERS

In the takeover of public schools, a considerable amount of collateral damage has been underreported, as most of the mainstream media has chosen to report unfounded success as touted by school reformers. However, following the money always tells the story. School district costs are usually the largest part or a close second in the budgets of most cities. And while the New Orleans school district had more than its share of fiscal problems before Hurricane Katrina, the fiscal mismanagement under the state and private charter boards has been unprecedented.

The district's funds are managed by a state board composed of eleven members, only two of whom live in New Orleans or its metro area. Nevertheless, they make decisions for the city's public school district, with a budget that exceeds $400 million. The board does not meet in New Orleans but in Baton Rouge—over eighty miles away—which also limits citizen input.

From the beginning of the state takeover, the citizens of New Orleans have been left totally out of the process. For example, citizens of New Orleans have never seen an RSD annual budget, unlike the people living in every other school district in the state. For the past twelve years, the citizens of New Orleans have never been given an opportunity for public comment on how tax dollars for public education have been spent. The RSD, a publicly funded school district, suddenly changed to a private institution. This lack of transparency and public participation in the public education process has serious implications and sets a dangerous precedent of eliminating the public voice of mostly poor and minority citizens. As communities across the country are fighting against voter suppression like in New Orleans, the education reforms have been successful in totally removing the vote as it relates to public education from the citizens of New Orleans.

And in the last decade, there have been repeated instances of corruption, malfeasance, and criminality related to school funding in New Orleans. In October of 2005, after amending their contract with then state education superintendent Picard, director Bill Roberti of the consulting firm Alvarez and Marsal secured $10 million in change orders of construction jobs without the New Orleans School Board's approval.[36] Change orders in construction contracts that exceed a certain amount must be approved by the OPSB to ensure that the contract will be completed without running over budget. The $10 million change order signed by Roberti far exceeded that threshold. In March 2006, Alvarez and Marsal signed a $29 million contract with the Recovery School District to oversee the rebuilding of schools in working with FEMA from New Orleans that was acquired by the state in Act 35. This was essentially the same contract that Alvarez and Marsal signed with the Orleans Parish School Board for the same school buildings in October 2005 for $24 million.[37] With that, Alvarez and Marsal were paid twice for the same work. On April 20, 2006, the Louisiana Board of Elementary and Secondary Education (BESE) approved a contract to hire Teach for America to provide 125 teachers for New Orleans and southeast Louisiana for $468,468.00. The contract was backdated to June 1, 2005.[38] The backdating of this contract allowed Teach for America to be paid during a period it did not have a contractual relationship with the state of Louisiana.

At the end of the 2006–2007 school year, Guidry and Associates, a firm contracted to provide security for RSD in New Orleans, was paid over $30 million to provide security to fewer than thirty schools and the central office, even though security for 2004–2005 for 120 schools and central offices was less than $13 million. Security costs skyrocketed after Hurricane Katrina. Before Katrina, the OPSB spent about $46 per student for school security. In 2006–2007, RSD spent $2,100 per student on security. Astonishingly, the RSD paid more than 425 percent above the nation average. In the 2008–2009 school year, the RSD direct-run schools spent $690 on security per student—fifteen times pre-Katrina spending on school security.[39] Transportation costs also skyrocketed, because charter schools had all-city attendance zones, unlike neighborhood schools. Before Katrina, the New Orleans public schools transportation budget was a little over $14 million for 123 schools. That cost has risen to $35 million for fewer than seventy schools.[40] It is very clear that these costs are way above market rate, and that many contracts were awarded without a bid process.

Additional examples of fiscal mismanagement and corruption:

In February 2010, the former business manager of Langston Hughes Academy pled guilty to stealing over $600,000 from the charter school by making more than 150 cash withdrawals from Hughes' operating account over 15 months. The theft was discovered in the organization's annual audit. The employee was sentenced to five years in federal prison and ordered to pay over $675,000 in restitution.

In December 2013, New Orleans police charged a former New Orleans Military and Maritime Academy business manager with stealing $31,000 by writing checks that were invoiced as if they were to office supply stores but were really to a non-profit he controlled.

In 2011, an employee of Lusher Charter School's accounting department embezzled $25,000 by forging five checks she wrote to herself from the school's bank account. The school discovered the theft and it was reported in its annual financial audit.[41]

The charter schools in New Orleans have a sweet deal. All of them charge the state an indirect cost, which can be as high has 21 percent—for many schools that equates to $500,000 to $2 million per year. Indirect costs may include an administrative fee from a fiscal sponsor for handling a grant, what many call bookkeeping for an organization that does not have the capacity. And in New Orleans, the charter schools operate in public school buildings (many of which are new, paid for with tax dollars) where they *pay not a dime in rent*. Additionally, under legislation passed a couple of years ago, all repairs of buildings are paid out of our tax dollars starting in 2018, even the cost of repairs of public buildings that are used as profit centers.

In January 2016, the state's legislative auditor issued a scathing report on the management of every state agency. The Louisiana Department of Education was cited for not monitoring student enrollment, accounting for a loss to taxpayers of more than $1 billion.[42] With that, school districts were paid for students who may not have been enrolled in schools resulting in that lost revenue. School districts annually received funding from the state based on enrollment, so reporting enrollment inaccurately by school officials can cost the state or result in school districts not having enough funds to service its student population. In this case, the lack of monitoring of enrollment accounted for a loss of $1 billion to the state, which annually has budget shortfalls. Of course, this seems to be business as usual, given the lack of regulatory monitoring by the state department of education. The legislative auditor's report also revealed that the RSD was cited for the ninth straight year for failure to locate millions of dollars in property in its inventory—each year RSD officials promise to correct the problem, but they never fix it.

The fiscal mismanagement does not end there. After Katrina, FEMA awarded $1.8 billion to the Louisiana Department of Education to renovate and rebuild schools in New Orleans. This is a large amount of money for any school district, but especially so in New Orleans, where so many school buildings were in bad shape even before Katrina. The RSD controlled most of the buildings, and it received most of the money to rebuild and/or renovate schools. Yet, in a 2012 report, the legislative auditor found waste and mismanagement. Some architect and engineer reports do not sufficiently inform RSD of the progress and quality of work, and potential change-order credits to RSD are not always adequately pursued. Change orders were approved with overhead and profit that is greater than the 10 percent allowed by the contract, and change orders were approved with items that cost more than local construction market standards.[43]

In 2014, RSD officials announced that the New Orleans's $1.8 billion school-facilities rebuilding plan would have to be scaled back due to a budget gap that could total $330 million—threatening officials' goal of putting every public school student in a new or renovated building.[44] Over the years, the Reverend Willie Calhoun Jr. of the Ninth Ward School Group and other activists voiced numerous concerns about the rebuilding process and the lack of community involvement. Before the budget shortfall was even announced in the newspaper, Calhoun and others anticipated at least a $300 million shortfall; they predicted a lack of oversight and difficulty completing such an ambitious building plan. In announcing the $330 million dollar shortfall, RSD officials said it was related to increased construction costs and an under-projection of student enrollment. Since Hurricane Katrina, RSD officials always maintained that enrollment would never reach pre-Katrina levels and that the city would have a smaller footprint; however, in explaining the shortfall, RSD officials announced that they need 3,800 elementary school seats more than projected and needed to cut 2,500 high school seats. To underestimate construction costs and student enrollment by $330 million is unacceptable; this blunder will keep thousands of students in inadequate schools. The $330 million shortfall could have possibly built seven new schools.

It is notable that the usual government watchdog groups have been silent on the rebuilding of schools and on the poor fiscal management of the RSD and several charter schools since Hurricane Katrina. Such groups were fiscal hawks when the OPSB managed the schools. Leading community oversight was the Bureau of Governmental Research (BGR) and the daily *Times-Picayune*, the city's largest newspaper. Both were at practically every school meeting, ensuring that the school board followed policy, and both routinely made recommendations— especially related to finance—to the school board and media.

Since the 1930s, the BGR has provided oversight of all government agencies in New Orleans. On its website it describes itself as an independent, nonprofit, nonpartisan organization that is dedicated to gathering information on government and other public issues.[45] Over the years, it has been a constant critic of the school board. For example, it led the charge for an audit oversight committee that reviewed and critiqued the board's process and policies monthly. After Katrina, it continued oversight of every government agency in metro New Orleans but has been strangely silent on the public schools in New Orleans. In the past, the massive fiscal improprieties at the state Department of Education and the RSD that have been documented by the Louisiana legislative auditor would have been reported by the BGR, with calls for drastic changes.

The New Orleans Office of Inspector General, created after Hurricane Katrina, has also been silent on the fiscal mismanagement of the public schools. Like the BGR, its mission is to make sure tax dollars are spent wisely and according to policy. It claims it is responsible for eliminating corruption, fraud, and abuse, and for holding government officials accountable, to ensure efficient and cost-effective government. Since the office opened in 2006, it has been out front as the city's official fiscal hawk, pointing out problems and making recommendations. But it is silent on public schools, ignoring its legal responsibility.[46]

A PRIVATE PUBLICLY FUNDED SCHOOL DISTRICT

More than twelve years after Hurricane Katrina, the reformers have been successful in taking our most important public service, public education, from the public and reestablishing an inequitable school system that offers drastically different education services to children based on race and class.

Today the scam is in full play. Charter school boards rule in the land of public education with unquestioned authority. They are still making unfounded claims of academic success with unreliable data, and those claims are basically still accepted by the mainstream media. The local and national philanthropic community still provides charter schools with millions of dollar annually, even as New Orleans charter schools continually perform worse academically than every other school district in the state of Louisiana. And the charter school movement is as strong as it has ever been politically, with one of the most powerful lobbies of any special interest group in state and local government. It has control of the state education board, the state superintendent, and the local school board.

Fraud is embedded throughout these reforms, even in the wording of the original legislation. The original 1995 Louisiana charter school law and Act 35 describe the legislation as an experiment, yet no policies or practices that are components of an experiment have been implemented for more than twenty years.[47] For example, there is no evidence of a stated hypothesis, permission granted from parents, a description of the study, or all the components that are included in an experiment since the charter school law's inception. Since the opening of the first charters in the 1990s, such schools have not had the semblance of a "thoughtful experiment." There have never been any rational steps taken for schools to reach some conclusions about public education: efforts were not made to develop a hypothesis, record observations, or make deductions to arrive at conclusions.

The latest reform victory is a policy that passed the state legislature in 2016 permanently removing the public from the public education process. Just as in Act 35, Act 91 establishes special governance procedures for only the city of New Orleans. Act 91 basically neuters the OPSB, as Act 35 did in 2005. It gives the charter school board unchallenged authority, without any interference from the OPSB, and gives OPSB only limited participation in the approval, extension, renewal, or revocation of charters on the recommendation of the superintendent. It also permanently establishes former governor Blanco's executive order after Hurricane Katrina, which removed all provisions within Title 17 of the Louisiana Revised Statutes requiring approval of faculty and parents for creation of charter schools and relating to their participation in the operation of a charter. This essentially puts authority for the creation and management of charter schools under the full jurisdiction of the unelected charter school board.

With practically no authority over charter schools' operations, policies, and practices, the OPSB and the public are still liable for charters' operations, policies, and practices. For example, the OPSB mandates the OneApp lottery process and guarantees charter schools' ability to accept students citywide, while the legislation eliminates neighborhood schools.[48] Act 91 continues the inhumane massive transportation of students across the city starting at 5:30 a.m. daily. Act 91 gives regulatory oversight to a thirteen-member appointed advisory board, with nine members from charter schools and/or the Recovery School District. This advisory board, by way of Act 91, has the authority to implement a process for the transfer of schools from RSD back to OPSB and to determine funding for government functions, and the board has the authority to stop the transfer of schools back to OPSB if it determines the process is not following the law. The advisory board has more power than the duly elected school board and in many ways acts as the duly elected board instead of in an advisory capacity. The authority given to this advisory board sets a precedent.

New Orleans offers invaluable lessons to the country regarding the privatization of public education. Despite the alternate universe described by the education reformers, the reforms have been a total dismal failure and prove once and for all that the solution promoted by Milton Friedman and others for years for improving public education does not work. Following the hurricane, New Orleans charters received significant financial support, driving per pupil expenditures over $20,000, while many school districts in Louisiana spend less than $10,000 per student. New Orleans had the optimal conditions for success and millions of dollars, yet it still failed, consistently performing academically at the bottom compared to other school districts across the state. The New Orleans education reforms also prove that the real motive behind the reforms was removal of the public from the public education process, to shift control of the resources and student enrollment.

The inherent, fundamental problems of New Orleans charter schools raise several questions communities should consider when they weigh privatizing public education: Are charter schools driven by mission or profit? If they are driven by mission, are they fundamentally grounded in equity and access, and do they add value to public education as a collective effort? If charters are not rooted in missions based on equity and access, then it is likely you are looking at predatory academies, such as those that dominated the disaster in New Orleans.

Kristen Buras, a professor at Georgia State University, in an article for the *Harvard Educational Review*, argues:

> New Orleans charters are less about responding to the needs of racially oppressed communities and more about reconstruction of the newly governed South—one in which white entrepreneurs (with black allies) capitalize on black schools and neighborhoods by obtaining public monies to build and manage charter schools.[49]

Post-Katrina New Orleans blew it. It had the opportunity of a lifetime to finally create the optimal learning environments for all kids in its public schools. This opportunity could have very well resulted in systemic reforms needed to help children who had historically been disadvantaged within its public school system.

As we look back at the rebuilding of New Orleans public schools after Hurricane Katrina, it is clear that the city's leadership was not interested in creating a school system that served all children equitably, regardless of race or class. Its mission was to reinforce the tiered school system that existed pre-Katrina and expand that inequitable system, reestablishing practices and policies that existed before the Supreme Court *Brown* case of 1954 and since *Plessy v. Ferguson* in 1896.

The education reforms mean that New Orleans offers vastly different educational services to students based on race and class. In many cases, particularly in some of the charter schools that use the "no excuses" model, the reforms offer no educational services to hundreds of poor and minority children. The reforms in New Orleans have had the same effects Jim Crow had on African American citizens after Reconstruction, in that they took from citizens/children rights that had been afforded them since *Brown*. As the Jim Crow laws of the late 1800s for all practical purposes put African Americans back into slavery, the education reforms in New Orleans put the citizens and students, a majority of whom are African American, back into a position where they have no role in the governance of public education.

The New Orleans public school landscape is a trip back in time, in which a cadre of white people who don't look like the majority of the student population or who don't send their children to public schools manage all the district's resources and decide what children go to which schools. After decades in which New Orleans had a democratically controlled public school system, the white power structure finally got it back, and it is in full control.

Charter Schools and the Event of Educational Sharecropping

AN ALTERNATE TAKE ON
THE CHICAGO PHENOMENON

David Stovall

As a hub for global finance, advancements in information technology, and management of systems of production, Chicago has fashioned itself as a viable competitor for investment from transnational global firms in business, industry, and entertainment.[1] It has also positioned itself on the frontlines of corporate education "reform" in the United States, relying heavily on state apparatuses that aim to replace public education with market-driven ventures.

Central to this vision are "public-private partnerships" and "choice," political devices that provide the illusion that students, parents, and families can access better options and outcomes away from traditional public schools. In fact, I have suggested that entities like central school offices, charter management organizations (CMOs), and state agencies use popular rhetoric and sophisticated marketing tools to solicit buy-in from parents and community members, stirring up what I call the *politics of desperation.*[2]

Racially and economically marginalized groups—already contending with uncertainty in education, employment, and housing—are targeted for intense recruitment efforts, but charter schools offer them only "more of the same." Currently there is no state or national evidence to support the conclusion that charter schools outperform neighborhood public schools.[3] Instead, what we are able to detect is that, despite the appearance of being fair, the lottery system of admissions is not random and can exclude certain students from admission, simultaneously boosting achievement outcomes.[4] When students who may struggle on standardized tests are not admitted, it heightens the capacity of the school to post inflated outcomes. Exclusion of certain students who are determined likely to perform poorly on standardized tests (mostly those who are differently-abled or who are English-language learners) is a strategy meant to ensure that charters have the best chance of admitting students who will not negatively affect the school's achievement data.

Moreover, missing from prevailing perceptions of charter schools and school choice are the realities of white supremacy, neoliberalism, disinvestment, mass displacement, hypersegregation, and the politics of disposability. Consequently, as charter schools portray themselves as viable for families that have been marginalized by the system, we are often presented with the direct opposite as the reality. In Chicago, as in New Orleans and New York City, corporate CMOs provide false narratives of success, bolstered by inflated data, while continuing to exclude a significant portion of black and Latinx families, especially those with children who are English-language learners or who are differently abled.

The discussion of the charter school phenomenon in Chicago may seem to account for a highly specific iteration in the schools' expansion throughout the city. But if we take time to understand how corporate charter schools are positioned as the viable alternative for black and Latinx families that have been "failed" by the system, a comparison to debt peonage—also known as sharecropping—is not far-fetched. While some may see my assessment as a departure, it is actually in concert with historical analyses of educational systems that have been positioned as being beneficial to black and brown life but which actually serve to undermine it. This "new" iteration of debt peonage we see with the proliferation of charters should be seen as a continuation of black and brown subjugation in the name of "progress." In light of the sordid history of human alienation of people of color in schooling systems in the United States, I hope to peel back the layers of an institution that does not produce the "results" promised to people of color in urban centers.

ROBBER BARONS, LANDOWNERS, AND SCHOOL CHOICE IN TWENTY-FIRST-CENTURY AMERICA

The comparison of corporate charter schools in Chicago with debt peonage/sharecropping was spurred by a conversation I had with a mentor and colleague, Bill Ayers, who referred to the processes engaged by corporate charter school systems as "educational sharecropping." When I asked him to explain, he observed that under the debt peonage/sharecropping systems of the Jim Crow South, families were given the idea of potential land ownership if they could save enough money to purchase land through the sharecropping system. Many African Americans were coerced and tricked into sharecropping in this way; they were made false promises about opportunities that never materialized.

In similar fashion, parents who are "sold" on charters are often compelled by the argument that they will reap greater educational opportunities, such as admission to selective enrollment high schools and to college, with accelerated options for success in the workforce. Yet, despite the promise of the afore-mentioned opportunities, many families endure a completely different experience. Some charters expect families to sign contracts requiring parents to monitor homework and to keep student performance high. In some instances, the contract has parents agree to a "nondisciplinary" dismissal, in which students are removed from a school for recording two consecutive failing grades in a subject. Many parents sign this agreement unaware of the consequences, thinking the charter school presents an opportunity for a quality education. Instead, a fake bill of goods leads to further isolation and marginalization.

Pauline Lipman and Cristen Jenkins succinctly compare the relationship of corporate charter school management organizations to the class of robber barons following the Civil War:

> Corporate philanthropy has historically played a significant role in shaping U.S. education to serve capital accumulation, social control, and White supremacy. Following the Civil War, foundations launched by "robber barons" used their newly acquired wealth to shape a colonial Black education system in the South that was central to the development of racially stratified labor markets in the United States.[5]

If we substitute "corporate philanthropy" and "robber barons" with "charter management organizations," it illuminates a dynamic that is unfolding in Chicago and throughout similar urban school systems. Driven by corporate interests and austerity budgets, corporate philanthropy in the form of major donations to CMOs supports a newly envisioned colonial education system, with Chicago operating as an epicenter of corporate school reform. As of the 2014–15 school year, charter students made up 14 percent of students in Chicago Public

Schools (CPS), including 23 percent of high school students and 11 percent of elementary students,[6] compared to New York City, where charter school students are almost 20 percent of the district, and New Orleans, where charters make up 84 percent of the city's schools.[7] Charter proponents seek to strengthen their base in Chicago, as CMOs subscribe to the idea that education is the newfound "marketplace," positioning families as the new gentry of consumers.

Feminist scholar Susan Mann provides an excellent description of the system of debt peonage. Her clarity and detail in explaining the debt peonage/sharecropping system creates room for the comparison with charters:

> Indeed, the failure of radical land reform, the demise of any hopes for "forty acres and a mule" and a continuing concentration of land ownership resulted in a strictly controlled system of production and marketing. Sharecroppers had little control over which commodity was produced and sometimes had little control over their labor, depending on the amount of assets . . . in turn usurious credit arising from the crop-liens system often locked sharecroppers into a system of debt peonage.[8]

Just as sharecroppers were forced into labor relationships where they had little control over their labor, families are given few options about how they can be involved in the daily life of a charter school—corporate charters often have few options for parent leadership and participation in school governance. Instead, like sharecroppers, parents can sign contracts that limit their ability to contest any action taken against students, including expulsion. These contractual agreements create loopholes that allow charters to ensure high test scores by forcing out "problem" students, an imperative as many charters have pledged to maintain test scores that "meet or exceed" benchmarks established by the state. This is certainly true in Illinois where, at many charters, students may be dismissed under the "nondisciplinary dismissal" policy. CMOs consider the policy representative of a "tough love, no-excuses" shift toward parental accountability, but little attention is paid to students who are removed from schools in an effort to boost test-score performance and achievement data reported to the district. In these instances, appealing to families' desperation for quality education results in deleterious effects. These issues must be brought into broader discussions of education reform.

As Mann describes, after the Civil War, the "radical land reform" of Reconstruction would have been to award forty acres and a mule to each formerly enslaved family, but sharecropping was positioned as a more amenable "reform," resulting in a socioeconomic system that closely mirrored slavery and lasted well into the twentieth century. In public education, the analogous "radical reform" would be community control and equitable distribution of resources for the most underserved and under-resourced schools. Instead, similar to the "compromise" made to the formerly enslaved individuals following the Civil War, charters have been positioned as the "moderate" solution by school districts and state and federal government. Included in this framing is a supposed "choice" for families that may amount to little more than a shiny new bow on the same garbage can filled with putrid waste. Despite external appearances, the same marginalization and exploitation await once you decide to look beneath the surface.

Like landowners, corporate charter leadership is staunchly resistant to labor organizing and unions. Just as landowners in the sharecropping system worked to oppose any form of collectivized labor in the Jim Crow South, corporate charters prevent teachers from collectively standing against labor exploitation and work to marginalize teacher voice. While there have been successful efforts to organize teachers in charter networks in Chicago, the largest networks (including the Noble Network of Charter Schools, for example) stand firm in their opposition to teacher unionization. Similar to the situations in New York and New Orleans, Chicago unions have been positioned as a major impediment to improved public education, as they prevent corporate charters from "innovating" toward longer school days and mandated unpaid overtime. For this reason, corporate charter schools prefer short-term laborers over educators who will remain in their teaching positions. Simultaneously, charter school networks seek teachers from the pool of alternative certification programs (e.g., Teach for America, New Teacher Project, Relay). They can safely anticipate that these candidates will remain in their positions for shorter amounts of time, as the alternative teaching certification programs advertise post-teaching employment opportunities after the required two years of service to the program. Corporate charters employ this recruitment strategy, as teachers who remain in their positions for shorter periods are less expensive to the state and district because less money is vested in their pensions.

Where sharecropping operates as a racialized market-based system, corporate charters operate in a similar fashion. Corporate charters secure contracts with cities, and the majority of their students are people of color from working class/low-income families. In addition to charters' profits from contracts with city governments, there are secure contracts for charter "partners" to service the school. For example, the network known as the Chicago International Charter Schools (CICS) has fifteen schools; instead of operating as a network with a centralized administration, each institution is an independent contractor of CICS. Similar to a corporate franchising system of fast-food restaurant chains, each charter school "operator" (their version of a principal) licenses the use of CICS curriculum and agrees to be advised by CICS on issues of curriculum, budget, and discipline. The CICS website details this relationship.

> Chicago International Charter School partners with School Management Organizations (SMOs) to facilitate the day-to-day operations at CICS campuses. The SMOs hire staff and faculty, provide professional development services, and manage the schools for performance results. This structure allows the campus, campus director and teachers to focus on our scholars and build school culture.[9]

Among the fifteen CICS campuses, there are four smaller SMOs (Charter Schools USA, Chicago Quest, Civitas Schools, and Distinctive Schools) that operate under the CICS banner. Their licensing agreements with CICS allow them to maintain independence within the network while potentially operating under a different set of rules. Even within the four SMOs, Chicago Quest operates via the Civitas Schools network, positioning it in a subcontracting relationship, similar to the way a housing contractor might hire another company to complete a task that it may not have the immediate resources to address. This market-based, subcontracting business model of education is viewed as "innovative" in that costs are trimmed by contracting services for students in the network's schools. At the ground level, if a family is looking for any type of accountability for problems that arise within the CICS network, it would seem the family would have to navigate a considerable labyrinth of management.

Explained succinctly by education scholars Michael Fabricant and Michelle Fine in their discussion of corporate charter reform, corporate CMOs have capitalized on a void in the provision of quality education for low-income/working class families of color.

> In the charter campaign, we hear echoes of the subprime mortgages nightmare and the recurring corruption of for-profit, higher education proprietary institutions. All of these iconic stories haunting communities of color as politically backed, market-branded "solutions" to long festering problems of the unequal distributions of private and public resources and structural racism within housing and education. . . . Charter schooling is expanded and presented as the answer to the public education crisis with little attention paid to evidence of academic outcome, fiscal accountability and equal access. The nexus between economic gain—be it administrative salary or profit-making—and the proportion of public dollars that reach the classroom is largely ignored.[10]

Key to the comparison of charters and sharecropping systems, as highlighted by Fabricant and Fine, is a set of views and values that deeply permeate the charter mission statement, in relationship to the students they propose to serve. In this particular market-based relationship, families and students are positioned as disposable. Because they can be displaced at any given time, they are similar to sharecropping families, who could be moved off plots of land at the whim of the landowner. Often, few reasons are offered for the subsequent forced removal of students.

Just as capital is accumulated through city contracts, black and brown bodies are accumulated in schools through paternalistic means. Charter schools press the narrative of public education's failure, drawing families into a system that conditionally welcomes them, while simultaneously discarding a significant number of students deemed "unsuitable" for the charter experience. Similar to the way landowners issued fake contracts to sharecroppers to allow them to "purchase their way out" of the debt-peonage system, charters dupe parents into believing that charters present the best options for their children. Consequently, the message communicated to families and students by corporate charter networks is "you are here for our use—if you don't shut up and take what we give you, then good luck on the streets." Of course, no one in any corporate charter management organization will admit this, but the stories shared by my colleagues suggest otherwise.

THE NEOLIBERAL RATIONALE OF PUBLIC GOODS IN CHICAGO

As documented extensively in the works of scholars such as Lipman, Kenneth Saltman, Fabricant, and Fine, Chicago has long been a hotbed of corporate educational reform.[11] In 1971, Mayor Richard J. Daley (father of former mayor Richard M. Daley) spearheaded a policy and planning initiative known as the Chicago 21 plan, which targeted twenty-one geographic and political districts (commonly known as "wards") for redevelopment. In an attempt to reduce white flight from the city, the mayor's office sought to devise a plan that would halt the exodus while securing development for the central business district. Because the populations of these twenty-one wards had shifted to either black or Latinx low-income or working-class families, the policy identified those groups for removal or confinement to the outer regions of the city. Considered part of the last wave of urban renewal strategies of the twentieth century that sought to curb white flight from large cities, the Chicago 21 plan should be understood as a hallmark of neoliberal reform in the city. Discussed in detail for the remainder of this section, the push to isolate and marginalize low-income/working-class people of color under the façade of providing viable educational options has become the norm in Chicago and other urban centers.

In the mid-1990s, a series of policy changes placed control of CPS more solidly in the mayor's hands. In Chicago, the mayor has sole authority to appoint the nonelected school board, which is responsible for development and approval of budgets, curriculum, and contracts, and for the construction of new schools. The current board of education for CPS consists largely of people from business, legal, and philanthropic sectors. This arrangement fosters reciprocal relationships between the board and the mayor's office, as board members are usually individuals or employees of organizations that have contributed significantly to the mayor's reelection campaign, or to local charter networks. Furthermore, the mayor, as final arbiter of school decisions, can overturn any decision made by the board or a local school. Facilitated by the twenty-two-year mayoral tenure of Richard M. Daley, and extended under Mayor Rahm Emanuel, a blueprint for numerous cities in the United States was created by Chicago in which education "entrepreneurs" decentralized the school system through market-based competitive strategies.

While many tout these changes as positive, a deeper interrogation reveals they have largely resulted in the further marginalization of low-income and working-class communities of color. Deepening this marginalization is the fact that the State of Illinois has operated without a budget for over two years (2015–2017). This has resulted in drastic cuts in social services and education. As part of a midyear budget cut, CPS was forced to trim $46 million.[12] Governor Bruce Rauner is in a stalemate with the legislature concerning budgetary matters while drug treatment centers have been closed, mental health centers have been shuttered, and higher education at state schools has been deeply compromised. Indeed, instead of "justice-minded reforms," these budget decisions should be described as "neoliberal austerity." Decisions in this vein are largely rooted in the belief that free-market economies provide solutions to the vast majority of social concerns and, like other neoliberal reforms, they have centered on the rights of the individual, not the collective society. The idea of the market as "self-correcting" underlies rationales supporting privatization of public goods as a way of achieving cost-effectiveness and maximizing profits, and as a means of improving options for those traditionally excluded from market transactions, including low-income families of color. Because the resources on offer in the marketplace are falsely positioned as being equally available to all people, low-income and working-class families of color are blamed for not accessing them.

In education, a central part of such strategies is a belief that competition will ultimately boost academic performance. Under free-market capitalism, the idea is that if one school performs well, its success will push others to improve or close, as families "choose" better education providers and drive down enrollment at subpar schools. However, in reality each school serves a different set of students that requires a unique set of resources. Neoliberal competition-based models are predicated on schools as sites of efficiency and replication; such models foster patterns of exclusion, as "winners" (i.e., schools where students score high on standardized tests) are championed while losers (i.e., schools with students who score poorly on standardized tests) are subject to further marginalization or termination.

CHARTER SCHOOLS IN CHICAGO: VARIANCE
AND A FAILED VISION

In the mid-1990s, a small number of charters were started by community organizations and former independent schools. In Illinois, charters were originally positioned as options for parents who wanted a small-school environment for their children, where teachers collectively concentrated on pedagogy. Similar to the original vision of Al Shanker (former president of the American Federation of Teachers), charters were positioned as a public school option where teachers could learn from each other through examples provided in an actual school. Known as "mom-and-pop" charters in Chicago, they functioned as spaces for teacher collaboration and curricular innovation, and cooperated more closely with the Chicago Teachers Union (CTU) and public schools at large. Unfortunately, this vision of a network of small, cooperative, and innovative schools was completely lost as charters began to shift to a neoliberal corporate frame.

I first heard of charter schools in the late 1990s. As a graduate student at the University of Illinois at Urbana-Champaign, I had become familiar with a community struggle around quality education. Residents were trying to find a way to address inequality in the town's school district after a scathing 1996 district audit by a group of researchers from Michigan State University. The audit revealed that black students received 66 percent of suspensions but were only 20 percent of the district's population. In conversations with community members, I began to hear murmurs about starting a charter school. At first I didn't understand the concept—I couldn't comprehend the fact that the state would be willing to put up 70 percent of the operating costs, with the charter responsible for raising the remaining

30 percent, without some type of quid pro quo relationship. Given the state of corruption in Illinois (the only state with more incarcerated elected officials is Louisiana), I thought it was another scam allowing some corporation to launder money, using schools as the conduit. Community members assured me this wasn't the case. Even though the charter never came to fruition in this small town, the idea stuck in my head as an option for educators, parents, and students.

When I returned to Chicago from graduate school in 2000, I noticed that there were a couple of independent charters in the city, and a set of charters that appeared to be run by members of a larger conglomerate organization. The aforementioned CICS was one of the first charters I heard of, and it had multiple campuses. Before I came to know the terms "charter network" or educational management organization, I knew of a set of charter schools that shared black, white, and yellow signage with "Chicago International Charter Schools" at the top of the logo. Two of its schools were in buildings that were former Catholic schools in the predominantly black neighborhood of Englewood. At the time, there was little data compiled on the "success" of charters, as they comprised just a small portion of schools, and many thought them to be a new form of alternative education.

The independent charter schools were created mostly by members of community organizations, former public school teachers, and administrators of CPS schools. It was a short-lived dynamic, and many of these independent "mom-and-pop" charters were picked up by larger networks, or were closed after a few years of operation. Most charters rented buildings from either CPS or the Archdiocese of Chicago, and many were starved of resources, due to the difficulty of raising the remaining 30 percent of operating costs. The majority of these independent charters shut their doors by the mid-2000s—around the time that CPS began its first significant round of school closings in 2004—and were quickly replaced by corporate charters, whose administrators used the premise of educational innovation and school choice. Meanwhile, CICS began expanding its network, as did the Noble Network and the UNO Charter School Network.

As the larger networks began to emerge, charters were positioned by CPS and political leaders as a cost-cutting option in an age of austerity budgets. During lean times, resources are even more concentrated in wealthy communities, and public funding for education and other social services come under greater scrutiny. Under the façade of "innovation" by way of "educational entrepreneurship," charter networks are able to parlay this reality by securing contracts with the district. Competition-based models, such as charters, fuel this cycle, with their supporters backing initiatives such as teacher merit pay for student performance. This process undermines the ability of teachers' unions to engage in collective bargaining, and allows charters to propagate a narrative that market competition is good for families who want "choice." This was certainly the case in Chicago, where the CTU faced staunch opposition from the mayor's office as it defended collective bargaining rights. Although the state budget crisis is largely a manufactured crisis, corporate charters are able to sell the state of Illinois on the supposed cost-efficiency of charters. Strangely enough, charter schools in Illinois remain an urban phenomenon, as they specifically target black and Latinx neighborhoods throughout Chicago and the outlying suburbs. Poor white students in rural areas in the state have not been the target of CMOs, as their districts do not see charters as viable options for their communities. There is a racialized component here, in that only black and Latinx students are deemed to be in need of "repair," unlike their white suburban and rural counterparts. In a form of educational sharecropping, only black and Latinx families are targeted for participation in a system that is sold as advantageous for their children.

CMOs use a number of marketing techniques, including elaborate orientations for families of prospective students, accompanied by perks (e.g., raffles for computers and tablets). All of these strategies are used to draw families in while developing rationales to dismiss students or to prevent teachers from organizing. In the absence of critical questioning, both small and large networks are able to strengthen their grips in communities that are historically underserved.

Instead of contributing to wholesale academic improvement, these new instruments of reform are creating an entirely different dynamic, as witnessed by students and families in cities like Chicago. With the new proliferation of charters, those who have historically experienced the greatest levels of marginalization and isolation are all but guaranteed to experience even more. Called the three Ds of Chicago school reform, destabilization, disinvestment, and disenfranchisement are rampant in the aforementioned communities. Furthermore, elements of the Chicago model of corporate education reform have been duplicated in cities including New York and New Orleans. Chicago and New Orleans even shared a chief executive officer (or superintendent) in Paul Vallas, who shepherded neoliberal policies in Chicago from 1995 to 2001 and in New Orleans from 2007 to 2011.

Ideological shifts have had profound implications for public education in Chicago, home to the third-largest public school system in the United States. The Civic Committee of the Commercial Club of Chicago, a group of business interests, developed a 2003 report known as *Left Behind*.[13] It advanced the argument that students in the United States were falling behind those in Southeast Asia and western Europe in reading, math, and science. The authors suggested a retooling of the Chicago Public Schools through an infusion of "innovations" from the business sector, in an effort to strengthen the workforce and return the economy to supremacy in the global marketplace. Consequently, it was argued that business leaders, not educators, were best suited to foster the most productive changes, as they were most knowledgeable about strategies for boosting competition among education providers.[14]

ENTERING THE CORPORATE CHARTER ABYSS— EXPOSING THE POLITICS OF DESPERATION

With Arne Duncan (who would later serve as secretary of education) at the helm of the school system, the city moved forward with policy recommendations suggested in *Left Behind*, rolling out a plan in 2004 called Renaissance 2010. CPS proposed to target up to seventy "chronically underperforming" schools for "transformation" by 2010 into a hundred schools with the designations of charter, contract, or performance school. While charters are granted by the state, contract schools allow individuals or groups that have secured contracts with the city to create schools. Contract schools are a close cousin to charter schools with regard to funding formulas, but the distinct difference is a direct partnership with the city, rather than the state. Currently, the largest contract institution in Chicago is the Academy for Urban School Leadership (AUSL), founded in 2001, with thirty-two schools in operation.[15] AUSL is not a charter network per se, as it has contracted with CPS to provide "turn-around services" for schools that are experiencing chronic underperformance. When a school is "turned around," the entire faculty and administration are fired and replaced. AUSL, as an "academy," partners with universities to train new teachers and administrators to serve in the turnarounds. Schools in the "performance category" aim to give principals and teachers some autonomy regarding curriculum and schedule. They are still under the direct auspices of CPS, in that they are completely funded by the district. Importantly, the intent behind scaling these schools up was to reduce the city's financial obligation to free public education.

The continued gouging of black and brown students by charter networks has only deepened the politics of desperation in the city. In a city that is steadily losing its black population (178,000 black Chicago residents left the city between 2000 and 2010), many charter schools located themselves in immediate proximity to neighborhood public schools, often plucking off students who did not have learning disabilities or who were not English language learners. I have had personal experiences with this dynamic through ASPIRA, a charter network with four schools in Chicago serving primarily Latinx students and communities. ASPIRA's extraction of students from a local neighborhood school in this instance was rooted in geography and confusion. I was invited by teachers to the Helge Haugan ASPIRA campus in the Albany Park neighborhood on Chicago's Northwest Side. After I parked my vehicle and walked over to the building, I read the marquee—Haugan Elementary—but I couldn't find the entrance. Fortunately, I knew a member of the maintenance staff, whom I encountered working outside on the school grounds. After we greeted each other and caught up, I asked him if I was at the Haugan ASPIRA campus. He laughed and smiled at my question, and told me that we were standing at the Haugan CPS campus and that the ASPIRA campus was around the corner.

After we parted and I continued on my way to the school's front door, I reflected on the fact that Albany Park is a neighborhood of first-generation immigrant families who rely heavily on community networks for advice on making adjustments to their new environments. The existence of two schools with the same name, located around the corner from each other, serving students of the same age and grade level must cause quite a bit of confusion to new families in the area. The advantage of the ASPIRA campus is heightened by its newer building, which may signal to some parents that the education provided in the building is "better." New residents in this community, many of whom are in the process of learning English, may face numerous challenges in choosing a school.

Another revealing example is the network of charter schools known as Urban Prep Academies. Currently a small network of three charter schools operating on Chicago's South and West Sides, its claim to academic success is a 100 percent college admissions rate for its graduates, all of whom are young black men. (The struggles of two Urban Prep students in their journey to college graduation are chronicled in the 2016 documentary *All the Difference*.) Urban Prep gained national support for its efforts, but the undercurrent also deserves discussion. In public conversations about Urban Prep, I often offer a warning that a critique of a network that specifically serves young black men automatically positions you as a naysayer of black education. Given the gratuitous structural violence encountered by black men on a daily basis, any critique of Urban Prep is met with intense rebuttal. However, because of my proximity to and concern for former students and former teachers, I believe the network's strengths and weaknesses warrant discussion.

When an institution claims a 100 percent college-going rate, a number of questions should be raised. For example, parents scramble mightily to get their sons admitted to the school, but Urban Prep leadership rarely addresses the issue of attrition. The 100 percent college admission rate is a problematic assertion. The wording on brochures and in advertising is misleading. It would be more accurate for Urban Prep to report that 100 percent of its students who make it to senior year are admitted to college. However, this qualifying language does not appear in its marketing literature, continually preventing parents from asking what happens to students who do not make it to graduation, a critical question. Additionally, there are worthwhile questions about how many students leave in their first two years at Urban Prep.

In another revealing instance, a group of Urban Prep teachers held a press conference in 2015 to publicize their attempt to organize a union and combat teacher turnover through transparent employment agreements and collective bargaining. Despite broad support from students and some parents, their efforts to organize were thwarted by Urban Prep leadership. Urban Prep continued to present itself as "student-centered," yet the committed and popular teachers who led the organizing efforts did not have their contracts renewed for the 2016–2017 school year. The message was clearly communicated: "upstart" teachers would not be tolerated, and personnel decisions would be addressed only on an individual basis.

Continuing the robber barons' legacy is the curious case of political operative Juan Rangel. As a longtime ally of the Daley and Emanuel mayoral regimes, Rangel parlayed the efforts of the former community organizing group known as the United Neighborhood Organization (UNO) into one of the city's largest charter school networks, UNO Charter School Network (UCSN, also commonly referred to as UNO). Before its foray into schools, UNO was a community organization focused on civic engagement and economic development. As a charter school operator, it ran sixteen schools with over eight thousand students. Rangel is known for firmly positioning himself as an assimilationist, and for focusing UNO's curriculum on the "Americanization" of Latinx students. In many UNO schools, families are drawn into open houses with mariachi bands, and the school highlights Mexican culture in other ways, such as having students wear a uniform similar to the ones worn by students in public schools in Mexico City. But even as the schools attract many first-generation Latinx students, enrollees are not allowed to speak Spanish. Putting forward the idea that the schools are conduits preparing Latinx students for the workforce, the UNO network compels students to adhere to an "American dream," while exploiting the desperation of families seeking viable educational opportunities for their children. When charter or contract schools hold open houses and community presentations, parents and potential students understandably are drawn to the immaculate presentation of the physical plant. The newly scrubbed floors, new lockers, and professional presentation of the school by a young and energetic new staff are key factors in engendering a sense of desire and belonging. For many families, anything is better than what they have traditionally had at their disposal, especially as funding for traditional public schools is progressively chipped away.

Deepening the presence of the organization and charters in predominantly Latinx neighborhoods on the Southwest, West, and North Sides of the city, Rangel in 2009 secured a $98 million grant from the state of Illinois (under disgraced former governor Rod Blagojevich) to build new schools for UCSN.[16] At the time, it was the largest public subsidy ever offered to an organization to run charter schools. Between 2009 and 2012, Rangel poured money into the architecturally eye-catching UNO

Soccer Academy on Chicago's Southwest Side, a school modeled after soccer academies in Europe and South America that cultivate talent for premier European soccer leagues. But after community activists and families expressed dismay at how Rangel received the $98 million, the federal Securities and Exchange Commission also took an interest. It soon discovered that, in addition to securing the contract through his political connections, Rangel had a conflict of interest when he engaged one of his top deputies (who also happened to be a relative) to provide windows for the new school buildings via a $1.9 million no-bid contract. Rangel also tried to keep from the public his "business" expenditures—hundreds of thousands of dollars in travel (on the order of $60,000 per year) and lavish dinners (sometimes with thousand-dollar tabs) at Chicago's finest restaurants. Instead of serving jail time, Rangel paid a $10,000 fine. When he was dismissed as CEO of UCSN in 2012, he was given a $200,000 severance package. While UCSN has distanced itself from Rangel, his corrupt practices tainted the already dubious relationship between charter networks and city and state government.

DEEP POCKETS AND WHITE SAVIORS WITH BLACK AND BROWN ENFORCERS

UCSN and the Noble Network of Charter Schools (NNCS) are the two largest charter networks in the city of Chicago. While each network depends heavily on corporate giving to cover operating costs, NNCS has the boldest strategy for securing corporate dollars. NNCS partners with local corporate and nonprofit entities to "name" its schools. Currently, the Chicago Bulls basketball organization, DRW Trading, and current governor Bruce Rauner have schools with their names (a school was named after Rauner when he was a billionaire hedge fund manager). In full disclosure, my employer, the University of Illinois at Chicago, has a Noble-branded school connected to its medical campus.

More than 95 percent of the NNCS's student body is either African American or Latinx, residing on either the South or West Sides of the city. The network is headed by CEO Michael Milkie, and twelve members of the twenty-two-member board of directors are employed by multimillion-dollar corporations, including DRW, Northern Trust, LSV Asset Management, and the Exelon Corporation. With eighteen schools in the district, NNCS plays a major role in Chicago's public/charter debate.

Families are deeply drawn to its "college-going culture," but topics absent from discussions of its empire are the makeup of its teaching staff and its deeply punitive discipline policies. Like many charters throughout the country that serve students of color in urban centers, the vast majority of its teachers are white and hail from alternative certification programs, such as Teach for America and the New Teacher Project. Meanwhile, many of those responsible for discipline on its campuses are people of color. It has made a push to hire more people of color and NNCS alumni as teachers in recent years, but its discipline policies remain more reflective of prison culture than transformative practice.

When students are "out of compliance" with an extensive set of rules, they are given detention and fined. Parents United for Responsible Education, a community organization that calls for transparency and accountability within CPS, reported the NNCS collected $386,745 in fines from students between 2009 and 2012 for disciplinary infractions.[17] While the NNCS touts its role serving African American and Latinx students from low-income and working-class communities, students there are encumbered and kept from advancing to the next grade if fines are not collected.

Despite the exposé on the collection of student fines, the robber baron mentality of Milkie and the NNCS has a parallel in the sharecropping narrative, in the form of a deep-seated belief that black and brown youth need to be saved from themselves and that white saviors are the ones to show them the way. In this instance, parents are excluded from governance and leadership, and have little say in school curriculum and the hiring of teachers and principals. In 2014, when Illinois charters were seeking to change the law so charters received full funding from public sources, they gave students a day out of school and required teachers to ride buses to the capital and lobby legislators for the change in the charter funding equation. To further incentivize teacher participation in the effort, they gave instructors a certain amount of money for every person they got to accompany them on the bus to the capital to lobby for them. Because most charter teachers are not unionized, they can be docked pay or their contracts can be terminated if they don't participate in such actions.

The last of the major players in the Chicago charter empire is the University of Chicago Charter School. Even though it is a small network of four campuses, its influence is deep and broad due to its teacher incubator program, the Urban Education Institute (UEI). In 2000, after the University of Chicago decided to close its school of education (both undergraduate and graduate programs), its only research arm dedicated to education was the University of Chicago Consortium on School Research (popularly known as the Consortium). The Consortium has released numerous influential education reports since 1990, and in the same period the university sought to concretize a foothold in communities adjacent to campus or in close proximity to it. The University of Chicago is one of the primary landowners on the South Side, and it has been maligned for gentrification in the adjacent neighborhoods of Woodlawn (to the south of the campus) and Washington Park (directly west of campus). Not surprisingly, all four of the University of Chicago charter network schools are in gentrifying or gentrified neighborhoods. Providing schools in these communities may soften the blow of displacement and dispossession, since the charters may be seen providing community benefits to families that have experienced chronic disinvestment and marginalization. Ironically, all four schools are in shuttered CPS school buildings.

Despite the small footprint of University of Chicago charter schools, UEI has become the de facto college of education for the University of Chicago and the de facto pipeline system for charter school teachers. Currently its student-teacher placements are in charter schools, and the majority of positions for its teachers are in charter schools. Combined with the research arm, the university's charter school network has become a major force in the charter movement. The university is in the process of completing a multimillion dollar high school building, scheduled to open in the fall of 2017.

RESISTANCE AND THE FUTURE OF PUBLIC EDUCATION IN URBAN CENTERS

In spite of the velocity of change in the city, students, families, educators, and community members are not taking these events lightly. For example, UNO's teaching force unionized in 2016 and called for improved learning conditions for students (including the addition of counselors and nurses). The teachers sought cost of living adjustments to salaries and a reduction in mandated work hours. Using the argument that good working conditions are good teaching conditions, they were able to negotiate a contract that addressed some of their concerns.

However, the unionization of UNO teachers does not address the issue of charters supplanting neighborhood public schools. Austerity budgets remain the standard of the day, allowing charter networks to maintain their foothold in large urban districts. Even as no discernable data demonstrate that charters outperform public schools, the rhetoric of a failed public education system still has traction with the general public and with many families that have experienced disinvestment and marginalization in CPS.

Given the aforementioned realities, Chicago may be poised to make important interventions in the current charter phenomenon. Through the work of a coalition of community organizations and the CTU, Chicago became the first city to place a cap on charter school proliferation. Because charters have not been proven to outperform CPS neighborhood schools, community organizations along with the CTU demanded a moratorium on the development of new charter schools in the district, and the cap was included in the union's recently approved contract.[18] Despite the city's hypersegregation and the intentional marginalization of black and brown communities, resistance to the charter phenomenon is present and expanding.

A 2016 call by the National Association for the Advancement of Colored People (NAACP) for a national moratorium on charters created new opportunities to critique and debate charter expansion while engaging critical questions about what constitutes quality education. Charters nationally have systematically excluded differently abled students and English language learners, and the NAACP noticed that charters offer little transparency regarding budget and discipline policies.[19] While this assessment of charters is largely accepted throughout the ranks of the NAACP and the Democratic Party, the recent appointment of Betsy DeVos as secretary of education may stall the effort at the federal level. As the 2015 CTU report *A Just Chicago: Fighting for the City Our Students Deserve* makes clear, there is a broad relationship between systemic inequality and charters:.

> Students living in segregated neighborhoods with concentrated poverty, unemployment, and low wages have fewer opportunities to learn and are more likely to be affected by social policies like mass incarceration. . . . Years of school "reform" efforts in Chicago have resulted in the loss of successful programs, intensified racial and economic segregation, profound disruptions to communities across the city (particularly on the South and West sides), the loss of thousands of experienced teachers, and millions of dollars in school privatization expenditures.[20]

A combination of firsthand accounts—as more students, families, and former teachers share stories about their experiences with charters—and awareness of the realities of broad-based oppression have great potential for galvanizing resistance and changing conditions. Those of us who are working collectively to provide an alternative account of the current charter moment are confident that our efforts will not be in vain.

From Community Schools to Charter Chains*

NEW YORK'S UNEQUAL EDUCATIONAL LANDSCAPE

Terrenda White

> It's like the myth of Bethesda in the Bible, the myth that
> said an angel would come to a pool of water each year
> and the wounded [residents] who got there first would be
> healed. . . . The myth of Bethesda is in our community—
> places that give the myth of healing through competition
> but do nothing but taunt the greatest aspirations of those
> who have been broken.[1]

Walking down a busy street in New York City or riding
the subway from Upper Manhattan to a borough across
town, you'll likely see numerous advertisements for charter
schools. Indeed, glossy images of a new school are common at
bus stops, on billboards and trains, featuring pictures of happy
children in colorful uniforms accompanied by messages prom-
ising a "world class education" fit for preparation to enter the
best colleges.

Between 2005 and 2014, while living and studying in Harlem, I regularly passed these ads. I also spoke informally with

---

*I use pseudonyms for particular charter schools and individuals who par-
ticipated in my research study in order to protect their privacy.

neighbors, parents, and grandparents who were swayed by the carefully crafted messages of hope and opportunity. One day, on a slow bus ride across 125th Street, I observed a woman smiling as she gazed at an ad for a popular charter school. She said to me, "You know what? I finally got my son into one of those nice charter schools."[2] Later, while I was serving as a teacher's aide in a school in East Harlem, a parent explained to me his decision to enroll his daughter in a charter school for the coming year: "They just have way more resources, stuff I didn't have when my wife and me went to public schools in the city."[3] On yet another occasion, while I was working as an evening instructor with detained women on Rikers Island, a mother in my writing class shared her hope for her child's future, which was tied to access to charter schools: "I want my child to do better in life than me. . . . Luckily I got her into this nice charter school."[4]

After several years of spontaneous discussions about charter schools with neighbors, church members, and various community organizers, it was obvious that charter schools struck a nerve with hopeful parents seeking quality choices for schools in neighborhoods circumscribed by inequality and limited resources. It wasn't a stretch, therefore, when I decided to study charter schools for my dissertation at Teachers College, Columbia University.

What I learned is that, for the past fifteen years, the expansion of charter schools in Harlem mirrors the national story of charter school expansion, an effort initially embraced by innovation-minded local actors and educators but one that was eventually transformed to reflect the interests of market advocates focused on competition and bottom-line performance outcomes.[5] So, though a market vision of charter schools signals "change" in a neighborhood, systemic inequalities remain in the form of disparities in resources and of racial segregation between schools and communities. In some cities, disparities have worsened terribly during this period. Hence, while charter schools offer new possibilities for educational opportunity to a minority of hopeful parents, it is important to weigh the promises of charter schools against their outcomes and their impacts on every child. Doing so makes it possible to have critical hope, rather than competitive hope, and provides a systemic vision for collective transformation of public schools that serve all children and families, particularly in communities where equity has long been promised but little has been delivered.

Three neighborhoods have been centers for New York City's experiment with charter schools: Harlem, Central Brooklyn, and the South Bronx.[6] The racial composition of each neighborhood, with the exception of those affected by recent gentrification trends, is predominantly black and Latinx. The neighborhoods have rates of poverty almost twice the city average. White and affluent communities lie only blocks away. Amid the entrenched segregation by race and class, families, residents, and activists within these neighborhoods have launched historic struggles for educational equity and local control.[7] Many of those efforts were part of broader struggles for political and economic rights and for social and cultural recognition.[8]

Indeed, in the face of an often indifferent or hostile establishment of city leaders, business elites, and residents in affluent neighborhoods, citizens of Harlem, Brooklyn, and the South Bronx have fought bitter battles for inclusion and empowerment. There were integration efforts in the early-to-mid-twentieth century, local and community control movements in the mid-twentieth century, and legal battles in the late-twentieth century challenging the city's unequal school-finance system.[9] In the aftermath of each struggle, sometimes seemingly before the ink was dry on legal contracts and fragile bargains were struck with city and state officials, promises for systemic change and educational equity in New York City were broken. It is in the historical context of more than five decades of stalled policies and weak support for restructuring the city's racially segregated and unequal school system that ideas of choice and competition via charter schools emerged as new hopes, offering possibilities for change. In 1998, the state passed legislation for charter schools, known as the New York State Charter Schools Act. The law was designed "to provide opportunities for teachers, parents, and community members to establish and maintain schools that operate independent of existing schools and school districts," in order to improve achievement, expand opportunities for at-risk students, encourage different and innovative teaching methods, provide professional experiences for teachers, and expand choices for parents.[10] By offering unprecedented autonomy from a bevy of district rules and regulations, and by inviting local teachers and community members to open schools, charter schools presented a new path, and a renewed hope, for educational equity and local control.

Early hopes were likely fulfilled, as nearly all of the first groups petitioning for charter schools in the city, between 1999 and 2004, particularly in Harlem, were stand-alone charter schools that partnered with youth-development groups and arts-based initiatives. Among the early charters established in Harlem was the first Latino-led charter school in the state, which partnered with a progressive community-based organization.[11] The mission statements of these early charter schools described intentions to offer culturally and linguistically inclusive curricula, including dual-language programs, project-based and/or "field-based" learning in the community, and "real-world" problem solving, and expressed a desire to nurture the "whole child," with an emphasis on helping students in Harlem gain "cultural knowledge of their community."[12] Many of the city's first charter schools, moreover, included parents, teachers, and members of partner organizations as representatives or voting members on boards of trustees.

The first charter school to open in the state, Sisulu-Walker Charter School of Harlem, in 1999, served over two hundred children in kindergarten through second grade. Its mission included supporting the whole child by "nurturing their intellectual, emotional, artistic and social development."[13] Sisulu-Walker integrates Swahili-based phrases for classroom names that convey character principles related to courage and discipline. Over time, the school partnered with the local YMCA to offer music instruction, and it introduced students to local activists during annual events, such as "Breakfast with a Civil Rights Legend."[14] But while Sisulu-Walker was an independent stand-alone school, it contracted a number of support services from a for-profit education management organization (EMO) called Victory Schools, Inc.[15] Founding teachers and principals note, however, that the school maintained its independence from the EMO, which provided "vendor services" and did not have full executive authority of the school, a distinction that would prove important as private management organizations came to play a much larger role in the full management and control of charter schools in Harlem.

Indeed, as the city's charter sector expanded somewhat explosively between 2007 and 2012 to more than 150 schools spread across the five boroughs, nearly half of all charter schools in the city would come to be affiliated with or fully managed by EMOs and nonprofit[16] charter management organizations (CMOs).[17] CMOs operate networks of charter schools with common missions and instructional designs, and share central office support.[18] CMOs typically have support and financial resources from private donors, and are often founded with the intention of replicating.[19] Notable CMOs include the Knowledge Is Power Program (KIPP), Achievement First, Uncommon Schools, and Success Academy Charter Schools in New York. Some researchers describe CMO-affiliated charters as "franchise charter schools," due to the schools' often scrupulous attention to "brand," to bottom-line performance statistics, to image management, and to the standardization of school products and practices.[20] Over time, the predominance of franchise charter schools was evident in Harlem, as, by 2012, approximately twenty-nine of its forty-four charter schools were affiliated with just five CMOs.[21] With the support of political leaders, such as former mayor Michael Bloomberg (who espoused a staunchly business-oriented mind-set for improving public schools and courted business elites and foundation leaders to sponsor the opening of scores of charter schools), CMOs rapidly replicated charter schools in the city and initiated two-thirds of the total charter schools in the Harlem neighborhood.

As the number and character of charter schools in New York changed from independent, stand-alone schools founded by community groups to replicated schools affiliated with nonprofit management organizations, charter expansion remained highly concentrated in the city's largely black and Latinx neighborhoods of Harlem, Central Brooklyn, and the South Bronx. As such, while the city's charter sector served more than fifty-nine thousand children in 2013, approximately 60 percent of them were African American, compared to 30 percent of students in district schools who were African American.[22] Harlem alone contained nearly three-quarters of all charter schools in the borough of Manhattan.[23] Consequently, while charter school students made up only 4 percent of the city's total public school enrollment, charter school students in Harlem made up approximately 25 percent of its district enrollment.[24]

In a short period of time, the once heterogeneous sector of community-based charter schools shifted to become an expansive sector populated by privately managed schools in black and Latinx neighborhoods. Autonomous from district regulations, and capable of amassing enormous private capital from wealthy philanthropists, CMOs employ an army of senior managers, central office staff, and school coordinators to orchestrate school operations and budgets, including marketing, advertising, and oftentimes direct oversight of everyday classroom instruction via scripted lessons. Teachers in these schools are rarely unionized (teacher turnover rates on average are higher in CMO-affiliated charter schools compared to those of stand-alone schools and district schools). Moreover, local participation, in the form of community or parent representation (as voting members) on boards of trustees, is rare. And nearly all charter schools in the city are either highly segregated or "hypersegregated," as more than 90 percent of New York City charter school students are African American or Latinx.[25]

In this very different and rapidly concretizing climate, community groups and activists in Harlem, Central Brooklyn, and the South Bronx are now waging formidable battles against a charter sector that offered hope and the promise of change but instead has taught bitter lessons. In New York City, as in New Orleans, Chicago, and other cities across the country,[26] the charter school sector has failed to restructure basic relations of race and power in the control and governance of public schools, particularly in historically disenfranchised communities of color. Indeed, systemic efforts to restructure financial and racial inequalities between neighborhoods and schools has been abandoned or, in some cases, worsened.[27]

Tracking the broad trends in Harlem's charter sector over time, from the opening of the neighborhood's first charter school in 1999 to recent trends in 2016, we can see how a once heterogeneous sector of community-based charter schools shifted to become an expansive sector populated by privately managed schools. This shift has had profound consequences for teaching and learning inside charter schools, for largely black and Latinx children. The instructional programs of the early period of Harlem's charter movement, which emphasized dual-language programs and focused on helping students gain "cultural knowledge" of their community, have been replaced with "no excuses" practices popular of late, which emphasize behavior and frequent testing, and focus on results and assimilation to middle-class norms often predicated on deficit views of culture in communities of color.[28]

CHARTER SCHOOLS IN HARLEM

In less than ten years, having reached the cap on the number of allowable charters under the original legislation in 1998, legislators passed an amendment that raised the cap, allowing an additional hundred charters and thus ushering in a second phase of charter expansion.

In 2010, a third phase of expansion began, tied to efforts to secure grants from the federal Race to the Top initiative, which resulted in congressional approval of an amendment to yet again raise the cap for more charters. By 2012, New York was authorized to grant up to 460 charters, with more than 136 charter schools already in operation throughout the city, concentrated primarily in Harlem, Central Brooklyn, and the South Bronx.[29]

Each of the earliest charter schools in Harlem was a stand-alone school, typically serving grades kindergarten through two with plans to expand to grade eight. As stand-alone schools, they functioned independently from district rules and were governed by a single board of trustees with direct control over the financial, administrative, and programmatic operations of the school, including evaluations of the school's principal, oversight of the school's financing and budget, and supervision of the school's academic program. "Stand-alone" is a somewhat misleading term, however, because while most of the early charter schools in Harlem functioned with a single board of trustees, these schools often partnered with community-based organizations for special services. Those organizations, though, typically had a representative on the board of trustees and rarely managed or governed the full operation of a school. Two examples of such schools are Community Charter School (CCS) and Elevation Charter School (ECS).

When CCS opened, it partnered with a youth development program, while ECS, which opened a few years later, partnered with a community-based arts program. Each school had parents, teachers, and members of the partner organization represented on its board of trustees. Like nearly all of Harlem's early charter schools, CCS and ECS were housed in private buildings, sometimes in spaces affiliated with the partner organization or in small, affordable spaces leased by the school. Both CCS and ECS were "mission-driven"—they focused on providing special services to children, such as youth counseling services, access to the arts, or cultural activities intended to foster "knowledge of the community's cultural heritage." As school leaders at these mission-driven charters developed academic goals and curricular units for children, they relied on partner organizations to provide enrichment and support with special services and activities. An apt description of schools like CCS and ECS was conveyed by ECS's founders, who defined charter schools as "mission-driven and locally governed schools" that were intended to, as it was explained to me, "design a coherent school program that capitalizes on the strengths of the community in order to meet the needs of the students."

As New York approached its second phase of growth, the organizational qualities of a new crop of charter schools in Harlem differed from those of the original mission-driven, stand-alone schools. Brighton Charter School (BCS), for example, was neither a stand-alone nor a mission-driven school, and did not partner with a local organization. BCS represented a wave of schools that served elementary or middle school grades, with plans to serve a wider scale of students across elementary, middle, and high school, and operate multiple schools in different sites with the help of nonprofit CMOs.

Across the United States, CMOs can function in two primary ways: they can support charter schools as "vendors" providing operational services based on the particular needs of schools (e.g., payroll, accounting, legal, or financial services), or they can hold executive authority over the full management of schools, including such aspects as daily operational procedures and academic and curriculum development, as well as student assessment and data management or analysis support. Nearly all CMOs in Harlem[30] function in the latter capacity, holding executive authority over the full management of schools and their operations, with terms of service stipulated in business agreements with the boards of trustees of each school.[31]

Brighton, therefore, was one of several schools whose board of trustees contracted with a CMO for full management of the school. As a result, it shared back-office support, operational functions and routines, and academic or curriculum qualities with other schools affiliated with its CMO. Moreover, and unlike most stand-alone schools in Harlem's early phase of charter growth, BCS was "co-located" with district schools in a public building owned by the city's department of education. Significantly, this meant that BCS's managers and trustees didn't have to allocate funds to lease private space and could focus elsewhere, including on back-office support from a growing cadre of central managers who (ironically) were located in private office spaces in Harlem and in other areas of the city.

At its opening, BCS's CMO was relatively unknown in Harlem, as were many of its practices, including the use of formal recruitment and marketing strategies, such as posters, flyers, and newspaper ads. State documents for CCS and ECS report no formal recruitment practices in their early years; they relied instead on the strength of associations with community organizations and "word of mouth" among parents. For the most part, these strategies worked for CCS, which maintained a healthy demand among parents in its first years, boasting an admission waiting list of two hundred students, on average. ECS, however, struggled early on to generate sufficient demand, reporting approximately seventy-five students on its waiting list in its first three years and falling below enrollment targets each year after that. Some of ECS's struggles with enrollment were due to space limitations, since it had to split grades into two buildings. Unlike CCS, however, ECS was located closer to Brighton and several similar CMO-affiliated schools. The structural challenges ECS faced in finding a building to house all of its grades were later compounded by "market pressure," as both the number and type of schools around it changed, which fundamentally challenged its founders' early claims about charter schools' definition as mission-driven and locally controlled.

Community, Elevation, and Brighton charter schools represented important distinctions in the kinds of school choices available to Harlem parents during the early and middle period

of New York's charter expansion. CCS and ECS were proto-
types of early stand-alone, mission-driven charter schools that
partnered with community organizations and sought a vari-
ety of curricular and philosophical approaches otherwise not
represented in the neighborhood's district schools. Like most
charters in their "start up" years, each school struggled with aspects of school operation and with complying with state regulations. Yet not all the schools' struggles were the same, as some
faced major challenges to key elements of the schools' program
and major aspects of their respective missions. CCS's struggles
to secure space in an area of Spanish-dominant residents, for
example, impacted its core mission to provide dual-language
opportunities in Harlem. Similarly, ECS's struggles to recruit
and maintain teachers affected its co-teaching model and its
preference for innovative, teacher-created curricular units. The
assessment-oriented focus of central managers for BCS ultimately subsumed its focus on academic innovation, preventing its principal and teachers from developing new curricular
materials distinct from other schools in the organization. Surprisingly, in spite of such challenges and alterations, evaluators
and charter authorizers consistently deemed each school "true
to its mission."

A CHANGED CONTEXT: CHARTER CONSOLIDATION AND REPLICATION IN HARLEM

> *You remember in the old mom-pop hardware stores, you would
> go in and get a widget. And the old guy and his wife would go
> get [it], come back, and say, "How are your boys or your girls?"
> And you'd say, "Oh they're doing well." . . . Then Home Depot
> came and it wiped out all of the mom-and-pop stores and so
> everybody had to go to Home Depot. But Home Depot was not*

the same [experience]. . . . Everything was so neatly organized,
but you had to go into this giant warehouse to get this and that.
And people just did not really know you at Home Depot. Well
those trends seem to be happening [in Harlem] with our char-
ter schools.

—MATHEW YEATS, director of instruction
at a charter school in Harlem[32]

As New York reached its third period of charter expansion in
the second decade of the 2000s, not only did the quantity of
charter schools in Harlem grow but the types of charter schools
available expanded as well. The number of charter schools in
Harlem that were affiliated with CMOs, such as Brighton, grew
dramatically, outpacing the number of stand-alone charter
schools like Community and Elevation. These trends were tied
to patterns of consolidation and replication, a norm observed
in private industry and otherwise known as the "franchising"
and "Walmartizing" of products and services.

Changes in the state's education policies between 1999 and
2014 played a key role in local level changes in the neighborhood's charter sector. Former mayor Michael Bloomberg
gained control of the city's schools and rallied behind charter
schools, supporting the virtues of choice, competition, and accountability. Charter schools established after the mayor's restructuring efforts were often framed differently from schools
established previously (some early charter schools had even
denounced "competition" in mission statements about the
schools' goals and objectives). Stated objectives among early
charter schools aligned with objectives noted in the state's first
charter schools act, which held that charters would be created to
provide opportunities for groups, particularly teachers, parents,
civic leaders, and community groups. Charters were established

independent from existing schools and districts in an effort to expand learning experiences and opportunities for students most at-risk of academic failure; to encourage "different and innovative teaching methods"; and to create new opportunities for teachers and school administrators.[33] Their objectives did not exclude "expansion of choice" for parents or the importance of improving measurable results in student achievement on performance-based assessments. Taken together, however, early objectives made clear the importance of improving achievement for underserved students, primarily by freeing local groups to develop a range of learning opportunities.

During Bloomberg's tenure, charter programs and mission statements emphasized goals such as "to give students knowledge, skills, character, and dispositions" in order "to gain admission to competitive middle schools" or "to succeed in a competitive global economy." The language emphasized by newer charter schools in New York, therefore, also mirrored the rising focus on accountability policies nationwide.

State reforms also changed the participation of actors in the charter sector. While amendments to the 1998 state charter law prevented for-profit groups from establishing, operating, or managing charter schools, nonprofit groups were not as limited. These nonprofit groups were permitted to work in conjunction with teachers, parents, and community members and to marshal "all corporate powers necessary and desirable to carry out a charter program."[34] Revisions to the charter law in 2010, moreover, expanded these powers, by permitting the consolidation of separate charter school boards in order to facilitate the governance of multiple charter schools by one board. In this way, multiple boards of trustees across charter schools were allowed to incorporate into a single board (aka "incorporated boards"). State revisions to the governance structure of charter schools supported the expansion of CMOs in neighborhoods like Harlem, enabling easy replications of schools governed by single incorporated CMO boards.

FROM "MOM-AND-POP" TO "HOME DEPOT" CHARTER SCHOOLS, AND THE CONSEQUENCES OF A MARKET SHAPED BY PRIVATE INVESTORS

Despite the innovative potential of their schools, instructional leaders of stand-alone charters, also known as mom-and-pop charters, were up against political and market pressures that rewarded narrow approaches to student achievement and minimized the role of culture and student identity in teaching and learning. The growth and consolidation of CMO-charters over time, as well as punitive accountability policies that ranked schools based on test outcomes, rewarded the most aggressive and narrow forms of instruction, pressuring leaders on the ground to endorse more common approaches that were myopically data-driven and often culturally restrictive.

By the summer of 2013, nearly two-thirds of all charter schools in Harlem were affiliated with management organizations. These CMO charter schools were referred to by critics as "Home Depots," due to the larger scale of the schools and the CMOs' central control of school operations, as well as the schools' careful attention to marketing, brand development, and image management. Not only were "Home Depots" expansive, operating multiple schools across the community, city, and even the nation, but leaders in these schools often deferred to senior managers in central offices, who coordinated budgets, operations, and curriculum design and instruction too.

Indeed, in interviews with leaders of CMO schools, curriculum design and instruction were of primary interest to senior managers. Leaders described senior managers who, needing to manage multiple schools at once, implemented uniform instructional models across all schools. Principal Brenda Wynn, who led a CMO charter school, explained the appeal of uniformity: "[Our managers] believe in the replicable model. . . . So our curriculums are the same. Our literacy instruction is the same, our math instruction is the same. . . . There are little things that [leaders] can tweak, but there are certain things that are by design, and we are not allowed to change."[35] Wynn noted the frequency with which senior managers visited her school, announced and unannounced, and held virtual meetings with leaders in order to ensure uniform and efficient application of their instructional models across schools. "Our senior leaders have at least two to three meetings a week with us [about instruction]—whether they're on video or in person."[36]

Senior managers' control over curriculum and instruction was regarded as a trade-off by other principals of CMO charters, many of whom were relieved from the burden of operational tasks that principals in smaller schools might otherwise take on. "We don't have to worry about budgets . . . I'm not sitting in my office all day looking at budgets and approving this and approving that and worrying about the nurse and all that stuff."[37] Like Wynn, Principal Carrie Anderson is fond of her charter school and its national organization, particularly the enormous resources and supports for operations and professional development. While she acknowledged that her organization could be a "bubble" at times, and she felt restricted by the organization's national "brand" of instruction—which at times did not accurately reflect the diversity of her students' instructional needs—she valued the resources made available to her because of her organization's access to private capital.[38] Indeed, research indicates that prominent CMOs similar to ones in Harlem—such as the Success Charter Network, Noble

Network of Charter Schools, and KIPP—have greater access to large private capital, compared to public schools and smaller independent charter schools. KIPP, for instance, is able to provide upwards of an additional $5,700 per student, compared to the amount provided at independent charter schools.[39]

Yet access to private capital and resources, as well as freedom from having to coordinate budgets and operations, is not without consequence. Leaders at CMO schools in Harlem point to a lack of autonomy and control over instruction as a significant problem. Theresa, for example, began as an educator in a CMO charter and was promoted to assistant principal. While she acquiesced to the demands of senior managers, she was bothered by the organization's top-down hierarchical structure, which she described as devolving into forms of "bullying" with chronic reprimands of those who did not obey senior leaders. "The [organization] goes about this whole bullying tactic with teachers. Managers try to bully teachers into doing what they want. . . . But they should want people to do things because they see the value in it, not because they tell us to do it."[40] Private capital from investors, wealthy board members, or philanthropists, moreover, shape power relations between investors and school-level agents, often marginalizing the instructional approaches preferred by leaders on the ground.

Shawn, a founding dean of a CMO charter school, was almost certain that private capital pushed his charter school toward a data-driven culture characterized by myopic concerns for maximizing test scores. "The idea from donors was that 'We are giving [your school] all of this money, so where are our results?' But when money came, quality of instruction became diluted. . . . It was suddenly about structure and *quick, short* results!"[41] Shawn surmised that the more private investments his charter organization received, the more pressure there was to produce returns on such investments, in the form of high test scores. Shawn eventually left his CMO in search of a charter that fit with his professional ideas about teaching and learning. His departure, however, was due primarily to his disagreements with the data-driven rationales of senior managers. "My [former CMO] wasn't really about developing the whole child. They were about results. That's it."

Shawn, who spent nine years as a classroom teacher in Harlem before taking on positions in administration, tried to make sense of the difference between his instructional values and those of the managers of his former CMO. He described his own approach as "drawing from wells of rich knowledge" among students, particularly among students of color whose communities he believed had a history of resilience and hope, which fueled education endeavors for social change. As such, Shawn hoped to connect students to the historic meaning of education for social justice, a vision much broader than passing exams. "[History] shows that change is bigger than one plus one, or two plus two, or ten times ten. Students have to be able to draw from a well of rich knowledge that will keep them pressing toward the mark of the higher prize." Senior managers, however, had a different vision. Shawn was frustrated that, instead of drawing from the wells of knowledge from black and Latinx communities, managers instead were "digging for data" in order to raise test scores.

Shawn isn't alone. I met several dejected and frustrated leaders like Shawn who felt that "results" on their own did not serve as a meaningful driver of educational activity, either for himself as an instructional leader or for his students, whom he described as facing difficult social environments. For this reason, Shawn rejected data-driven practices, which he believed would not help students persevere through harsh environments or transform their communities. "I look at learning as building up students from within. I don't want to *quantify* them; I want to *qualify* them to be pillars of their community . . . so that *they* can impact the day and be an agent of change." Consequently, because of his different outlook, Shawn left the CMO charter. He felt like a "misfit" among senior managers who prioritized test scores above everything else.

However, not all leaders resolved differences with management by voluntarily leaving CMO charter schools. Some leaders are forced to leave, pushed out of schools because of clashes with senior managers regarding instruction. Charles, for example, was charged with overseeing math development for upper-elementary grades at a CMO charter school in Harlem and served as an instructional coach for math teachers across fourth, fifth, and sixth grades. Though he initially acquiesced to the data-driven rationales of senior managers, Charles was let go unexpectedly because of differences of opinion with fellow administrators. "We had a great reputation and many of our board members were famous and were millionaires and billionaires, but they operated from a business standpoint. So they were only looking at children's test scores or results, and to them teachers were either making results or not making results."[42] He noted with regret the disposability of leaders and educators who didn't follow data-driven rationales: "For those who don't look at the kids as being a product or a result . . . and wanted to help people grow [by] taking into consideration their different experiences, they were pressured to operate in a certain way or they were found replaceable."[43]

Charles eventually learned that he, too, was replaceable in the eyes of senior management. "I worked for the organization for three and half years, and my dismissal took two minutes."[44] Trying to make sense of his dismissal, he described more fully the conflicting rationales of senior managers and administrators. One episode involved his principal, who had hired Charles as a math leader and whom Charles described as having deep knowledge about educational processes:

> If [management] deems the school as not making results, then they'll want the principal to fire people, and my principal at the time refused to do that. He refused because he didn't feel as though it was the right thing to do. He didn't look at the kids as being a product or a result, and that's part of the reason I think, if not *the* reason, as to why he was eventually let go—he believed in helping people to become what he called "superstars" or growing. . . . So he had a lot of pressure put upon him to operate in a certain way and produce results in a certain way. And since he wasn't willing to adopt their system or their way of doing things, they found him replaceable.

Like his principal, Charles was terminated. Despite having a master's degree in math education, combined with enthusiasm and passion for the subject, as well as fond relationships with students and community members, Charles did not have his contract with the organization renewed. Though he was not "fired" for wrongdoing, Charles concluded that his termination was based on management's decision to hire math coaches who would aggressively carry out the test-driven instructional approaches of the organization.

Timothy Peters, a senior manager of a CMO, described having a sense of urgency to obtain the results that were expected by his organization's investors. As the director of pedagogy for a CMO in Harlem, Peters felt he earned his position because of his ability to "deliver" results expediently, which he believed satisfied the wishes of investors and charter founders. "Well, I've been involved from the beginning of this [CMO's] project. I'd say to the charter founders early on, 'So what kind of scores do you want this time around? Tell me what you want.' And then I'd say, 'Done!'"[45] According to Peters, the founders of his CMO were "big on data," and he felt confident that he could "move any kid" (in terms of test scores). Peters explained: "I'm probably one of the strongest educators in the city, because I can make the claim that I can move any kid's [scores]. . . . I bypass all those emotional issues with family problems and lack of security. . . . I do 'bypass surgery,' and I find a way to put students on the right track."[46] Peters's idea of putting students on the right track was almost wholly regarded as a "data problem," something easily "fixed" with explicit and urgent pressures placed on students.

Moving children's scores, Peters explained, required vigilance about students' test results. Students were often publicly ranked by their scores. Peters described the need for a behaviorist approach to efficiently "move" children's scores. Children had to "behave at high levels" to perform at high levels on tests:

PETERS: I first get [students] to *behave* at a high level. . . . No kid slips through my cracks! . . . And I'm not going to have any "1's" in my class!

TW: What if you do?

PETERS: Well, I'd know way ahead of time, and I'd fix it. . . . Our [CMO] has a very strong culture that's big on "who's got it" and "who's *not* got it" [scores based on data].

TW: And the students know this too—"who's got it and who's not got it"?

PETERS: Oh, yes they do!

For Peters, explicit ranking of students according to test scores (e.g., children were grouped in the following categories: "1's" were below average; "2's" were average; "3's" were proficient; and "4's" were above average) was necessary to promote competition, and the practice permeated the culture of instruction across schools in the organization. Good educators were defined as those who displayed, similar to Peters, a sense of urgency to "move kids" in terms of their scores.

Peters acknowledged, however, that urgency might detract from other forms of "moving" children, particularly in terms of intrinsic motivation and joy for learning. "When I get my kids' [scores] in sixth, seventh, and eighth grade, I don't have the time to be overly nice. . . . Perhaps that's one of my failings; I don't bring as much joy. I make joy suffer because of my urgency."[47]

Not only did the focus on test scores make "joy suffer," these approaches had sociocultural consequences for students, as test-oriented rationales designed to move kids' scores often meant restricting inclusive practices that were capable of engaging learners in more meaningful ways.

CULTURAL AND PEDAGOGICAL CONSEQUENCES OF SCHOOLS MANAGED BY PRIVATE GROUPS

In interviews with CMO leaders, test scores held symbolic meaning. Students' scores were treated as markers of character that were based on behavioral expectations associated with the cultural practices of dominant groups by race and class. Indeed, strict control of instruction by senior managers included the supervision of predominately Black and Latinx children's everyday behavior, including mannerisms, dress, language, communication, interaction, and presentation of self, all for the sake of "doing best on the test," according to one leader. In this vein, managers regulated certain nonacademic aspects of students' social and cultural lives that were viewed as *impediments* to test score production, and that required vigilance if they were to be "fixed." To explain, a leader of a data-driven school noted, "Many of our kids are coming from poor families, and have poor vocabularies, and have poor role models." Another leader noted similarly, "If students [in Harlem] had models of language, models of behavior, models that included ethics, principles, and character, rather than models that they see in poor neighborhoods, they would achieve better."[48]

Such heavy emphasis on the character and behavior of children in Harlem was tied to competitiveness on standardized tests. Camille Robinson, a former educator and current administrator in her CMO charter, explained what she believed was the organization's view of the relationship between behavior, character, and competition: "We don't just weigh heavy on the academics but also on the social stuff. Like one time I told a student, 'You smell bad and you need to wash up.' I know that's silly, but [students] need to know that because it makes them overall more competitive, not just academically but socially as well."[49] She went on to explain the daily vigilance regarding students' behavior:

> It's very strict. But I don't like to say strict because it has negative connotations. I just think it's very *orderly*. We have a specific way in which things need to be done. The mentality is that if you have order over the small things, then you won't have to worry about those things when it's time to "slam the exam." So we have students practice how to sit, what to do when the timer goes off, and just what to do when the time comes for the tests.

The inflexible and rigid norms demanded that managers communicate messages of passivity and conformity as paths to achievement and marketability. Principal Wynn noted, for example, that the aggressive push to improve children's test scores was intended to counteract stereotypes of poor children from Harlem. "I want people to look at my students as competitive, marketable, contributing members of society. I don't want somebody to look at my students and say, 'Oh, I'll give this kid a chance because they probably just came from a poor black single mother from Harlem.'" In contrast, Theresa worried that the rigid demands and constant reprimands students experienced in her school might undo the very hopes that Principal Wynn outlined earlier. "I think about what's missing. We're pushing [students] academically and our scores show that. But on a deeper level, if [students] do become successful . . . when they go to a dinner party, are they going to just sit in the corner?"[50] Theresa's concern touched upon the means by which students were made "marketable," means that fostered passivity, and ultimately undermined student's sense of power in the world to which they aspired.

Like Theresa, Charles was concerned that students were disempowered by the practices of his data-driven leaders, who he felt did not value the social worlds in which students lived and learned. Thus, Charles challenged the promotion of marketability and competition via conformity, and criticized the stigmatizing messages about the social and cultural environments of urban students, messages that presented them as deficient and in need of middle-class examples of success to which they ought to conform. "Educators are not supposed to make students feel as though historically their people don't function on the level as another group of people within the same nation.

You shouldn't make some groups *feel* inferior . . . but kids in Harlem are in just that sort of predicament."[51]

Contrary to his superiors' data-driven strategies, Charles turned toward progressive traditions of teaching. "Progressive teachers bring learning *to* the students, where they are . . . and they say to students, 'Your environment is the primary tool to get you to learn, so I'm going to start with the things that you see every day to connect you to learning.'"[52] Charles's description of progressive education utilized culturally relevant approaches to teaching, and he sought ways of valuing (and validating) the social worlds and cultural practices of students. He viewed these aspects of children's lives as *facilitators* for meaningful learning and connection to knowledge, rather than as impediments to test score production. In this vein, Charles lamented the practices of his former managers. "They were trying to show kids that they can learn [via high test scores], but they shouldn't separate students from their environment, or say to students that their environment is the problem." Instead, in a view similar to Shawn's vision of social change, Charles valued practices that promised not to "deliver children out of the 'hood'" by way of their scores but to cultivate meaningful connections to learning in hopes of empowering students to make critical changes within their communities, primarily by challenging the broader structure of inequality that circumscribed it.

Nonetheless, leaders like Shawn and Charles were pushed out of the CMO charters where they worked. Both were unable to fit into the narrow test-driven frameworks of senior managers who ultimately controlled instruction and framed achievement within rigid and stigmatizing cultural ideas about poor children of color. Theresa, however, found a way to transfer to another school within the CMO, one she described as "going against the grain" of organization policies. As an assistant principal at this particular school, she was able to "get away" with more flexible approaches that valued teacher input and the broader needs of students. She admitted, however, that her school's practices made it an outlier among the schools managed by the CMO, a feat she attributed to the school's location miles from central offices, in a neighborhood considered by managers as dangerous. "I think the [managers] are scared to come and visit us!"

A LOST VISION OF EQUITY: VOICES FROM EARLY COMMUNITY-BASED CHARTER SCHOOLS

As we've seen, early charter school leaders in Harlem weren't market-driven or motivated by competition with district schools to maximize test scores via highly rigid norms or narrow curriculum. These early schools were mission-driven, with deep ties to the community. Remarkably, several of these schools have retained their early vision, performing above the average of district schools and maintaining a stable force of teachers with low turnover rates. Although they draw little attention and often exist in the shadow of CMOs, the schools offer a lesson in their vision of equity, as minoritized voices but with perspectives that remind us what has been lost in nearly two decades of charter growth in cities across the country. The voices below belong to educators of color who work in the shrinking cadre of community-based charter schools that operate outside the purview of private managers, organizations, and groups. Indeed, several are among those who helped to start the charter movement in Harlem, yet they describe feeling marginal—like outliers in a movement they helped found.

"WE WERE THE BLUEPRINT"

Mr. Humphrey is sitting on the edge of a table, wearing a red shirt and black slacks. He is a tall African American teacher in his late thirties. "I'm from Harlem. I was born in Harlem; I went to school in Harlem. I love this community, and I love the rapport I have with people in the community."[53] A fellow teacher sitting next to him, Mr. Andrews, also an African American male, chimes in about his friend and colleague: "Yeah, we can go to the park right now, and you can't walk ten feet with [Mr. Humphrey] without people stopping to talk to him, or saying, 'Hey, I know him, that's Mr. H.' That's why people call him Mr. Mayor!" Together, Andrews and Humphrey laugh. Soon there is a short pause. Andrews continues, "But we should *want* that; we should want [kids] to be in a place like that. So that if a child is outside at ten o'clock at night, and Humphrey happens to be out there, he can say back to him, 'Hey, I know you! What are you doing out here? Where are you going?'" The men nod their heads.

On this morning, I am sitting with Andrews and Humphrey in the gymnasium of one of New York's oldest charter schools. The two men facing me have been with the school since its founding. When I first requested an interview with the teachers, they seemed surprised. In fact, Andrews shook his head, saying, "We were the blueprint, but [the media] won't even mention us. [Our charter school] doesn't have the million dollars backing us like Brighton or Excel Charter network, or the other big financial backers. But without us, there would be no them." I ask if there is ever collaboration between charter schools. Andrews answers, "I don't think collaboration is on this level." He pointed to the teachers in the room. "I think if anything, it's more the bigwigs who do it," he said, pointing upwards. "You rarely see teachers from another charter school come here, even just to look around and say, 'Hey, we're such and such.' It's a rare occurrence."

Our discussion with the men turns to policy, particularly shifts in the charter movement and the instructional significance for children in Harlem. I ask the men to share their thoughts about charter schools as a way of fostering competition and thereby improving school outcomes. Both men give a scornful look, and Humphrey answers slowly. He first explains his concerns that competition forces other schools to "wean" out troubled kids, students whom he believes are the most rewarding to work with over time but who take longer to succeed. He continues, evoking a community-oriented framework of charter schools that challenges notions of individual competition. "I think it's so important in a place like Harlem *not* to feel like it's a competition. . . . If [charter schools] could work together and gel things together, not only would students have much better performance but a much more sound community."

Soon, Humphrey's discussion of a community-oriented framework moves to open criticism of competition as a "corporatist" view, which he believes restricts flexible learning opportunities for students: "I feel that people just can't come to Harlem with a corporate mind-set and think that kids are going to connect to what they say." As Humphrey explains, the corporate mind-set profoundly limits educators' ability to address the needs of the children. He goes on, "With this profession, you have to be able to tackle things from different perspectives and points of view. You've got to really know the community you're going into. If you're not too familiar with the community, or the setting, it's going to be quite challenging, primarily because our kids face all types of challenges before they're even actually able to come to school. . . . So someone [less familiar] might come along and put a label on them."

Eventually, Humphrey's community-oriented framework evolved into a full critique of the social and cultural biases on which competitive instructional practices are predicated. This time the critique comes from Andrews, who explains his view of the instructional needs of children in Harlem as twofold— involving, on one hand, a struggle for students to discover their creative and imaginative selves, despite being racially and economically marginalized and subjugated, and, on the other hand, the need for them to learn how to compete in a broader world of much different, dominant cultural norms. For this reason, Andrews rejected a particular *kind* of competition, specifically, the brand of competition that is exalted at CMOs. This particular kind of competition is predicated on conformity and assimilation, and is not responsive to the duality of the academic endeavor for students in Harlem. He explained:

> In my family, learning how to be yourself was a big thing. We *strived* for that. My mother would tell us, "Don't you sit there and compromise yourself for everybody else. People have to learn to take and accept you for who you are, and if they can't, you better realize that it's their loss and not yours." . . . So, being competitive and losing a sense of yourself are two different things to me. You can still be yourself at a job interview; there's certain things you have to curtail of course. But I can put on a suit and talk to a CEO of a company, and if I'm outside hanging out with my friends, I'm not going to be talking the same way. Students have to learn how to turn things on and off. . . . As blacks and Latinos, it's like we've been taught not to be this or not to be that, and we've been

told to conform to this straight line—but when is the time for our kids to use imagination, to think, and to be themselves? I ask my students all the time to figure out the answer to the question, "Who are you?" If teachers just tell them to be one way, to compromise themselves for competition in the job market, that doesn't help with anything other than send the message that the people up there [*raises hand as if holding the top rung of a ladder*] have the right to control us down here [*lowers hand to indicate the bottom rung of ladder*].

I learned that teachers like Humphreys and Andrews are a minority, not only in terms of their race and gender, their ties to the community, or even their longevity as teachers in one charter school. They were also a minority in terms of their view of the charter sector and its purpose. Indeed, they were the only black teachers (indeed, black men) in their current charter school. They were also the only remaining teachers from their school's founding more than a decade ago. What stood out most, however, was their view of charter schools as *local* endeavors, meant to create contextualized and culturally flexible spaces for students "to be themselves" while preparing to compete in a world outside of Harlem. By resisting the notion that people "up there" should control the norms of students in Harlem, they didn't take for granted the social and cultural hierarchies that often frame learning and deny disadvantaged students access to culturally equitable schools. As we've seen in previous sections, these views are rare in a sector characterized by market pressure, which pivots on a bottom-line focus on competition and test-score production and rewards narrow instructional practices.

In the remaining section, I explore similar minoritized voices in a charter sector gripped by private groups and a market vision, to consider further the early and lost vision of equity that charters represented. Among the schools below, it is evident that alternative visions of equity exist, particularly among educators who viewed the cultural and linguistic diversity of their students as *resources* to facilitate, rather than impede, competition in a global society.

For example, Carl Rivers, the principal and cofounder of Elevation Charter School, one of the early stand-alone charter schools in Harlem, explained, "There was supposed to be one board for one school, and that board was to give all its attention to that one school. No longer did we have to deal with citywide initiatives affecting us, or that were made because of decisions and issues happening elsewhere."[54] When reflecting on replication and consolidation trends associated with the rise of CMOs, however, Rivers warned, "As CMOs grow, the supply of smart people, committed people, and multitalented people who were supposed to be devoted to one school diminishes, especially as CMOs add three to seven schools per year."[55] For Rivers, there were pedagogical consequences related to macro-level shifts in management and governance structure of charter schools, which mirrored problems associated with large bureaucratic systems. "Changes to the New York charter school law work to create an economy of scale on the governance level that starts to sound like a district, and it dilutes the quality of responsiveness to urban communities, and which contradicts the whole point of why we started a charter school."

Nina Reynolds is a parent and former teacher who was assistant principal at Jifunza Charter School, in West Harlem, which had implemented an alternative educational model that promoted dual-language learning. Reynolds described the school as parent-driven. "The parents run the school. I mean we think [administrators] run the school, but in reality, it's the parents' interests and the parents' desires that run the school. And as administrators we simply can't get away with unlawful demands and overly strict rules that may be used in other schools."[56]

Community Charter School, one of the early stand-alone charter schools in Harlem, not only maintained a unionized teaching force with lower rates of teacher turnover compared with those of nearby charter schools—and even with those of other district schools with unionized faculty—but also had a higher percentage of students proficient in English/language arts compared with students at nearby district schools between 2011–2012 and 2013–2014. Leaders at the school emphasized healthy and stable relationships between students and teachers, and sought to meet the emotional and developmental needs of learners. The school implemented a Spanish immersion program, and leaders encouraged children to be proud of their community and their origins. Indeed, Vivian Sheets, the principal of CCS, explained succinctly, "Yes, you have to be competitive to get into a top middle school, but you have to know who you are and know who the students are."[57]

Early charter school educators, therefore, spoke about competition and equity in expansive ways, reaching beyond test-result production, and taking seriously the social and cultural dynamics of classroom life as resources for deepening classroom learning and transforming sociocultural hierarchies in both school and society.

"WE ARE INSTRUCTIONAL DECISION MAKERS IN OUR SCHOOL": AUTONOMY AND CONTROL IN COMMUNITY-BASED CHARTER SCHOOLS

Independent, community-based charters have leaders who value charter schools because of the control and autonomy the schools offered to shape curriculum and instruction. While overwhelmed at times, these leaders refer to themselves as instructional "decision makers" and note proudly their visibility "inside the school building," rather than at distant locations in district or central offices. According to Paula Meyers, director of instruction at and cofounder of Elevation Charter School, autonomy from central agencies is important to ensure sustainable academic programs. "[Charters] were designed for innovation and autonomy. . . . So it's really good that we're localized and we have one board of trustees [because] there are decisions that we're able to make about the academic program that can have more continuity."[58] Meyers cherished the small-scale operation at her charter school, and felt that anything larger would "dilute the quality" of the academic programs there.

Charter school leaders like Meyers regarded charter schools not as competitors with, or indictments of, so-called failed public school systems, but as opportunities to make these systems more responsive to the public by addressing the local needs, challenges, and wishes of diverse students and parents, and offering a range of diverse instructional approaches to learning. Hence, leaders of independent charter schools in Harlem were wary of all forms of central control, including districts and CMOs, and instead described semi-horizontal relationships with faculty, parents, and community members. Sheets, for example, often stated to teachers and staff, "We're all in this together" to "make our little venture work."

Leaders of independent charters welcomed flexibility in instructional programs, a quality they viewed as essential to meeting the needs of their students. Meyers, for example, explained the importance of flexibility in the instructional model implemented at her school, which she described as constructivist in nature. "Doing [constructivist] programs involves muddling through, and talking, writing, and trying out the different strategies. It's a *process*. And it's very scary for teachers to see their students 'fail,' but I put that in quotation marks because it's struggling, it's not really failing."[59] Describing her school's ELA program, Meyers notes, "A scripted program cannot address our learners" because "it's too inflexible."[60] While she admits to using aspects of scripted phonics programs in the lower grades, she relies more heavily on flexible instructional programs in the upper grades. Mathew Yeats, like Meyers, was a director of instruction at an independent charter school, not far away from her school. He not only took pride in being able to change curricular models and adapt instruction to the particular needs of his students, he regarded this capacity as a fundamental characteristic of public school systems: "[Uniformity] is the corporatist way, but what gets lost in that kind of environment is personalization. What happens to teaching the whole child when you have a vision that says, 'This is how *we* do it [as a private organization], and this is how students have to be in order to stay in [our organization]'?"[61]

Flexibility and responsiveness across independent charters was balanced, however, with continuity and sustainability of instructional practices, a feature that leaders attributed to a localized and decentralized management structure. "We really wanted the freedom to stay the course with one instructional program," noted Meyers. Instructional leader Anthony Charles, who left his CMO (involuntarily) and accepted a new position as a coordinator for math instruction at a community charter school, compared his experiences: "Going from a big CMO to a smaller charter school is like going from New York City to the South! It's much slower, but I feel [my principal] really cares about shaping a culture that has deep structures and systems and a more solid foundation."[62] Charles described his new principal as someone who cared about instructional process and thus teaching and learning. "The sense of urgency feels different here because there's a lot that we're trying to do, but there's a strong foundation that we're trying to build. So now my sense of urgency has changed, and I'm slowly implementing a process to make sure everything is lined up properly."[63]

Indeed, I've observed that leaders across independent charter schools in Harlem value flexibility and autonomy in decisions about instruction, both in efforts to strengthen instructional foundations with continuity over time and in responsiveness to diverse students who have been historically marginalized and underserved by public schools. The expansion (and franchising) of charter schools in Harlem by large CMOs with competitive rationales focused on test-score production via standardized, rigid practices rocked the core intent of the charter movement for independent charter school leaders.

THE SOCIAL AND CULTURAL SIGNIFICANCE OF COMMUNITY-BASED CHARTER SCHOOLS

The rationales for participation in the charter sector among leaders of independent charter schools had social and cultural significance for black and Latinx students in particular. While specific instructional approaches to improving students' educational experiences varied across independent charters, leaders noted that autonomy and control allowed them to shape classroom environments that they believed were responsive to the challenges and strengths of their racially and ethnically diverse student bodies. Some leaders described responsiveness that was informed by the input and active involvement of parents, while others encouraged teachers to develop responsive practices that were "culturally proficient" about the social identities and challenges of students at the school, and still others believed that adherence to a constructivist-oriented instructional model was responsive to children's cognitive capacities.

CONCLUSIONS AND NEXT STEPS

Early advocates and participants at charter schools in Harlem sought equity and supported goals that involved instructional innovation driven by local actors, community groups, and educators. In the intervening years, there have been dramatic shifts toward a centralized and consolidated sector of privately managed charter schools that are locked in myopic contests for test scores. Unfortunately, these schools overshadow community-based visions of equity that were rooted in cultural, pedagogical, and epistemological changes and risk perpetuating the myth that to address systemic inequality, we simply need to close test-score gaps on state assessments. With their "myths of competitive healing," market-driven charter schools and their bottom-line approaches to performance outcomes leave gaping disparities between black and Latinx schools and communities, both in their tangible resources, related to financial supports and materials, and their intangible resources, related to knowledge, history, language, and "community cultural wealth," which are perpetually excluded in everyday academic endeavors.[64]

Educators, researchers, parents, students, and community activists can play a critical role in pulling back the curtain on a charter reform effort that is gripped by competitive rationales of schooling, and in doing so simultaneously recover less dominant visions of charter schools, and of equity that modeled not only different understandings of *how* to foster achievement and learning in schools but also redefined *what* "counted" as worthwhile knowledge for children of color in public schools. By joining forces with broader social movements for antiracist, community-based, democratic public schools—including traditional public schools—community-based charter schools can more effectively mobilize against market forces that have distorted early promises of charter reform. Through coalitions centered on the collective empowerment of parents, teachers, and communities to control public schools via democratic localism, the promise of inclusive, multiracial, and financially equitable schools is a viable prospect.

Appendix

*Anti-Privatization/Pro-Public
Education Organizations*

FairTest

The National Center for Fair & Open Testing (FairTest) advances quality education and equal opportunity by promoting fair, open, valid, and educationally beneficial evaluations of students, teachers, and schools. FairTest also works to end the misuses and flaws of testing practices that impede those goals. FairTest's Assessment Reform Network is a national project created to support parents, teachers, students, and others who are working to end the overuse and misuse of standardized testing in public education and to promote authentic forms. *http:// www.fairtest.org/*

Network for Public Education

The Network for Public Education, founded in 2013 by Diane Ravitch and Anthony Cody, is an advocacy group whose mission is to preserve, promote, improve, and strengthen public schools for both current and future generations of students. The goal of NPE is to connect all those who are passionate about our schools—students, parents, teachers, and citizens. *https://net workforpubliceducation.org/*

Alliance to Reclaim Our Schools (AROS)

The Alliance to Reclaim Our Schools (AROS) is an alliance of parent, youth, community, and labor organizations that together represent more than seven million people nationwide.

AROS is fighting to reclaim the promise of public education as our nation's gateway to a strong democracy and to racial and economic justice. AROS believes that the best way to ensure that each and every child has the opportunity to pursue a rich and productive life is through a system of publicly funded, equitable, and democratically controlled public schools. After years of division, AROS is uniting parents, youth, teachers, and unions to drive the transformation of public education, shift the public debate, and build a national movement for equity and opportunity for all. *http://www.reclaimourschools.org/*

Journey for Justice

Journey for Justice (J4J) is an alliance of grassroots community, youth, and parent-led organizations. Our members are base-building groups organizing to win community-driven alternatives to the privatization and dismantling of public school systems. We are organizing in our neighborhoods, cities, and nation for an equitable and just education system, based on a belief in the potential of all children and the rights of parents, youth, and communities to participate in all aspects of planning and decision making. *https://www.j4jalliance.com*

Parents Across America

Parents Across America (PAA) is a nonpartisan, nonprofit grassroots organization that connects parents from all backgrounds across the United States to share ideas and work together to strengthen and support our nation's public schools. PAA serves as a network for parents to share their concerns, activities, and strategies, and it equips parents with the tools they need to advocate for progressive policies at the local, state, and national levels. *http://parentsacrossamerica.org/who-we-are/*

Parents for Public Schools

Parents for Public Schools advances the role of families and communities in securing a high-quality public education for every child. *http://parents4publicschools.org/what-we-do/chapters*

CITY-SPECIFIC ORGANIZATIONS

New Orleans

Justice and Beyond is a community organization created to fight for justice in the Greater New Orleans area. Justice and Beyond is organized around change and the fight for justice. It is not a formal organization but gathers people from many walks of life who have come together to fight the righteous fight. Since its existence, Justice and Beyond has been on the frontlines of many of the issues affecting the city and its residents, one of which is the privatization of public school post–Hurricane Katrina. *https://www.facebook.com/justiceandbeyondNOLA/*

Chicago

The Caucus of Rank and File Educators (CORE) is a group of dedicated teachers, retirees, paraprofessional school related personnel (PSRPs), parents, community members, and other champions of public education who fight for equitable public education and hope to improve the Chicago Teachers Union (CTU) so that it fights both on behalf of its members and on behalf of Chicago's students. *http://www.coreteachers.org/about/*

New York

New York Collective of Radical Educators (NYCoRE) is a group of current and former public school educators and their allies committed to fighting for social justice in the school system and in society at large by organizing and mobilizing teachers, developing curricula, and working with community, parent, and student organizations. NYCoRE comprises educators who believe that education is an integral part of social change and that work must go on both inside and outside the classroom because the struggle for justice does not end when the school bell rings. *http://www.nycore.org/nycore-info/mission/*

Related Reading

Jean Anyon, *Radical Possibilities: Public Policy, Urban Education, and a New Social Movement* (Routledge, 2014).

David Berliner, *50 Myths and Lies That Threaten America's Public Schools: The Real Crisis in Education* (Teachers College Press, 2014).

Samuel Bowles, *Schooling in Capitalist America: Educational Reform and the Contradictions of Economic Life* (Haymarket, 2011).

T. Jameson Brewer, *Teach for America Counter-Narratives: Alumni Speak Up and Speak Out* (Peter Lang, 2015).

Kristen Buras, *Charter Schools, Race, and Urban Space: Where the Market Meets Grassroots Resistance* (Routledge, 2014).

Anthony Cody, *The Educator and the Oligarch: A Teacher Challenges the Gates Foundation* (Garn Press, 2014).

Linda Darling-Hammond, *The Flat World and Education: How America's Commitment to Equity Will Determine Our Future* (Teacher's College Press, 2010).

Megan Erickson, *Class War: The Privatization of Childhood* (Verso, 2015).

Michael Fabricant, *Austerity Blues: Fighting for the Soul of Public Higher Education* (Johns Hopkins University Press, 2016).

Michael Fabricant and Michelle Fine, *Charter Schools and the Corporate Makeover of Public Education: What's at Stake?* (Teachers College Press, 2012).

Jay Gillen, *Educating for Insurgency: The Roles of Young People in Schools of Poverty* (AK Press, 2014).

Dana Goldstein, *The Teacher Wars: A History of America's Most Embattled Profession* (Anchor, 2015).

Jesse Hagopian, *More Than a Score: The New Uprising Against High-Stakes Testing* (Haymarket, 2014).

David Hursh, *The End of Public Schools: The Corporate Reform Agenda to Privatize Education* (Routledge, 2015).

Alfie Kohn, *What Does It Mean to Be Well Educated? And More Essays on Standards, Grading, and Other Follies* (Beacon, 2004).

Jonathan Kozol, *The Shame of the Nation: The Restoration of Apartheid Schooling in America* (Broadway, 2006).

Pauline Lipman, *The New Political Economy of Urban Education: Neoliberalism, Race, and the Right to the City* (Routledge, 2004).

Jal Mehta, *The Allure of Order: High Hopes, Dashed Expectations, and the Troubled Quest to Remake American Schooling* (Oxford University Press, 2014).

Katherine Neckerman, *Schools Betrayed: Roots of Failure in Inner-City Education* (University of Chicago Press, 2010).

Bree Picower, *What's Race Got to Do with It? How Current School Reform Policy Maintains Racial and Economic Inequality* (Peter Lang, 2015).

Diane Ravitch, *The Death and Life of the Great American School System: How Testing and Choice Are Undermining Education* (Basic Books, 2016).

Diane Ravitch, *Reign of Error: The Hoax of the Privatization Movement and the Danger to America's Public Schools* (Vintage, 2014).

Dale Russakoff, *The Prize: Who's in Charge of America's Schools?* (Mariner, 2016).

James Ryan, *Five Miles Away, A World Apart: One City, Two Schools, and the Story of Educational Opportunity in Modern America* (Oxford University Press, 2011).

Kenneth Saltman, *The Edison Schools: Corporate Schooling and the Assault on Public Education* (Routledge, 2005).

Eric Shyman, *Reclaiming Our Children, Reclaiming Our Schools: Reversing Privatization and Recovering Democracy in America's Public Schools* (Rowman & Littlefield, 2016).

Jose Vilson, *This Is Not a Test: A New Narrative on Race, Class, and Education* (Haymarket, 2014).

Vajra Watson, *Learning to Liberate: Community-Based Solutions to the Crisis in Urban Education* (Routledge, 2011).

Acknowledgments

FROM RAYNARD SANDERS: The real story around the education reforms implemented post Hurricane Katrina would not be told if it hadn't been for the efforts of thousands of students, parents, and community members who have been begging for educational equity, as well as fundamental justice, for children to no avail for more than twelve years. Their efforts to simply participate in a democratic process around public education will never be forgotten or lost in history. Special acknowledgments to Kristen Buras and Bill Ayers, who assisted greatly in making this project a reality.

Notes

NEW ORLEANS—RAYNARD SANDERS: *The New Orleans Public Education Experiment*

1. James Anderson, "The Historical Context for Understanding the Test Gap," paper, 2004, https://www.unc.edu/courses/2006fall/educ/645/001/Anderson%20on%20Test%20Gap.pdf.

2. Donald E. DeVore and Joseph Logsdon, *Crescent City Schools: Public Education in New Orleans, 1841–1991* (Lafayette: Center for Louisiana Studies, University of Southwest Louisiana, 2011), 16–17.

3. Ibid., 47.

4. Thomas H. Neale, "The Compromise of 1877," *North Carolina in the Civil War and Reconstruction, Learn NC*, http://www.learnnc.org/lp/editions/nchist-civilwar/5470, accessed April 28, 2017.

5. DeVore and Logsdon, *Crescent City Schools*, 81 and 91.

6. Keith Weldon Medley, *We as Freemen: Plessy v. Ferguson* (Gretna, LA: Pelican Publishing, 2003).

7. Nicholas Bauer, "Annual Report, 1902," in *Notations on Various Schools, 1901–1902* (New Orleans: Orleans Parish School Board Collection, University of New Orleans).

8. Christopher Cooper, "Old-Line Families Plot the Future," *Wall Street Journal*, September 8, 2005.

9. Leigh Dingerson, *Keeping the Promise? The Debate over Charter Schools* (Milwaukee: Rethinking Schools, 2008).

10. Brendan Miniter, "A Silver Lining?," *Wall Street Journal*, September 6, 2005.

11. Kim Holmes and Stuart Butler, *From Tragedy to Triumph: Principled Solutions for Rebuilding Lives and Communities* (Washington, DC: Heritage Foundation, September 12, 2005), http://www.heritage.org/homeland-security/report/tragedy-triumph-principled-solutions-rebuilding-lives-and-communities.

12. United Teachers of New Orleans, Louisiana Federation of Teachers, American Federation of Teachers, *"National Model" or Flawed Approach? The Post-Katrina New Orleans Public Schools* (New Orleans: Cowen Institute for Public Education Initiatives, November 2006), http://www.coweninstitute.com/wp-content/uploads/2010/03/AFT NationalModelorFlawedApproach.pdf.

13. Jane Hannaway and Paul Hill, *The Future of Public Education in New Orleans* (Washington, DC: Urban Institute, 2006), http://www.urban .org/sites/default/files/publication/51021/900913-The-Future-of-Public -Education-in-New-Orleans.PDF.

14. Ethel Julien, Eddy Oliver et al. v. Orleans Parish School Board et al., "Reasons for Judgment," Civil District Court for the Parish of Orleans State of Louisiana Division N Section 8 No. June 12, 2011. This document outlines the reasons for judgment by Judge Julien in the former New Orleans Public school employees lawsuit and gives an important timeline that led to the employee firing, which documents critical events around the takeover of the New Orleans Public Schools by the Louisiana Department of Education before and after Hurricane Katrina, and includes Cecil Picard's letter to Secretary of Education Margaret Spellings requesting funds for rebuilding public schools in Louisiana, September 14, 2005.

15. Ibid.; United Teachers of New Orleans et al., *"National Model" or Flawed Approach?*, which describes the events around the takeover of public schools in narrative format.

16. Julien, "Reasons for Judgment," 15.

17. Cecil Picard, Louisiana Department of Education, to US Secretary of Education Margaret Spellings requesting $2 billion to assist parishes with the damages related to Hurricanes Katrina and Rita. In this letter, Picard stipulates what the funds would be used for within the affected parishes.

18. Campbell Robertson, "Louisiana Illegally Fired 7,500 Teachers, Judge Says," *New York Times*, June 21, 2012, http://www.nytimes.com/2012/06 /22/education/louisiana-illegally-fired-7500-teachers-judge-rules.html.

19. Ibid.

20. Danielle Dreilinger, "U.S. Supreme Court Denies Teacher's Katrina Layoff Lawsuit," *Times-Picayune*, May 18, 2015, http://www.nola.com /education/index.ssf/2015/05/supreme_court_denies_katrina_t.html.

21. United Teachers of New Orleans et al., *"National Model" or Flawed Approach?*

22. Jeff Bryant, "The Truth About the New Orleans School Reform Model," *Education Opportunity Network*, July 30, 2014, http://education opportunitynetwork.org/the-dishonest-case-for-the-new-orleans -school-reform-model/, accessed May 25, 2017.

23. Michael Deshotel, "New RSD Propaganda Machine Whitewashes Dismal Performance," *Louisiana Educator* (blog), August 9, 2015, http://louisianaeducator.blogspot.com/2015/08/new-rsd-propaganda -machine-whitewashes.html.

24. Julian Heilig, "Policy Brief: Should Louisiana and the Recovery School District Receive Accolades for Being Last and Nearly Last?," *Network for Public Education* (blog), August 28, 2015, https://network forpubliceducation.org/2015/08/policy_brief_louisiana/.

25. Francesca López and Amy Olson, "Ten Years After Katrina, New Orleans' All-Charter System Has Proven a Failure," *In These Times* (blog), August 28, 2015, http://inthesetimes.com/article/18352/10-years -after-katrina-new-orleans-all-charter-district-has-proven-a-failure.

26. Andrea Gabor, "The Myth of the New Orleans School Makeover," op-ed, *New York Times*, August 22, 2015.

27. Danielle Dreilinger, "School Transfer Data Raises Questions About Accuracy of Louisiana Dropout Rates," *Times-Picayune*, October 3, 2014.

28. Mercedes Schneider, "John White's Two Sets of 2015 ACT Scores," *Mercedes Schneider's EduBlog*, February 21, 2016, https://deutsch29 .wordpress.com/2016/02/21/john-whites-two-sets-of-2015-act -scores/.

29. Excerpt from an anonymous letter sent from a parent to the author.

30. Jan Resseger, "New Orleans Model Is Not Such a Model After All," *Janresseger* (blog), October 6, 2015, https://janresseger.wordpress.com /2015/10/06/new-orleans-model-is-not-such-a-model-after-all/.

31. Frank Adamson, Channa Cook-Harvey, and Linda Darling-Hammond, "Whose Choice? Student Experiences and Outcomes in the New Or- leans School Marketplace," policy brief, Stanford Center for Oppor- tunity Police in Education, September 30, 2015, https://edpolicy .stanford.edu/sites/default/files/publications/scope-brief-student -experiencesneworleans.pdf.

32. Shakti Belway, *Access Denied: New Orleans Students and Parents Iden- tify Barriers to Public Education* (New Orleans: Southern Poverty Law Center, 2010).

33. Rick Jervis, "New Orleans School System Re-Educated," *USA Today*, September 24, 2006. http://usatoday30.usatoday.com/news/nation /2007-09-24-neworleansschools_N.htm.

34. Better Education Support Team, Lellelid Anna, and William P. Quig- ley, Civil Rights Complaint, 2014, available at http://media.nola.com /education_impact/other/4.15.2014%20Carver%20Complaint%20For %20Release.pdf.

35. Coalition for Community Schools Conscious Citizens Controlling Community Change Journey for Justice, Civil Rights Complaint,

2014, http://b.3cdn.net/advancement/24a04d1624216c28b1_4pm6
y9lvo.pdf.

36. "Reasons for Judgment."

37. Ibid.

38. Ibid.

39. Dameka Morgan, Elizabeth Sullivan, Families and Friends of
Louisiana Incarcerated Children, National Economic and Social
Rights Initiative, *Pushed Out: Harsh Discipline in Louisiana Schools
Denies the Right to Education* (New York: NESRI, 2010); *A Focus
on the Recovery School District in New Orleans 2010,* http://www
.coweninstitute.com/wp-content/uploads/2011/12/History-of
-the-RSD-Report-2011.pdf; author interview with Louella Givens
for *A Perfect Storm*, documentary in progress (dir. Phoebe Ferguson), 2013.

40. Author interview with Darryl Kilbert for *A Perfect Storm*, 2013.

41. Center for Popular Democracy and Coalition for Community
Schools, *System Failure: Louisiana's Broken Charter School Law* (May
2015), https://populardemocracy.org/sites/default/files/Charter
-Schools-Louisiana-Report_web3.pdf.

42. Daryl Purpera, Louisiana Legislative Auditor, *Key Audit Issues 2016
and Act 461 Report* (Baton Rouge: Better Information, Better Louisiana, January 2016), https://app.lla.state.la.us/PublicReports.nsf
/0EA9F8004453B13486257F3F006B822C/$FILE/0000C2E4.pdf.

43. Daryl Purpera, Louisiana Legislative Auditor, *A Compliance Audit
Report on the Recovery School District–Capital Construction Program*
(Baton Rouge: Louisiana Legislative Auditor, June 13, 2012), https://
app1.lla.state.la.us/PublicReports.nsf/989452071AA2634486257
A1B004E9A3E/$FILE/0002AD55.pdf.

44. Danielle Dreilinger, "New Orleans School Building Plan $330 Mil-
lion in the Hole," *Times-Picayune*, June 26, 2014, http://www.nola
.com/education/index.ssf/2014/06/new_orleans_school_building
_pl_1.html.

45. "Profile," Bureau of Governmental Research, 2016, http://www.bgr
.org/about/.

46. New Orleans Office of Inspector General, http://www.nolaoig.gov.

47. Louisiana Legislature, "Charter School Demonstration Programs
Law," Acts 1995, No. 192, §1, eff. June 14, 1995; Acts 1997, No. 477, §1,
eff. June 30, 1997, http://www.legis.la.gov/Legis/Law.aspx?d=80968.

48. Louisiana Legislature 2016, Act 91.

49. Kristen Buras, "Race, Charter Schools, and Conscious Capitalism:
On the Spatial Politics of Whiteness as Property (and the Unconscio-
nable Assault on Black New Orleans)," *Harvard Educational Review*
81, no. 2 (2011): 296–331.

CHICAGO—DAVID STOVALL: *Charter Schools and the Event of Educational Sharecropping*

1. J. Smith and D. Stovall, "Coming Home to New Homes and New Schools: Critical Race Theory and the New Politics of Containment," *Journal of Education Policy* 23, no. 2 (2008): 135–52.

2. D. Stovall, "Against the Politics of Desperation: Educational Justice, Critical Race Theory, and Chicago School Reform," *Journal of Critical Education Studies* 54, no. 1 (2013): 33–43.

3. Erica Frankenberg, Genevieve Seigel-Hawley, and Jia Wang, *Choice Without Equity: Charter School Segregation and the Need for Civil Rights Standards* (Los Angeles: Civil Rights Project/Proyecto Derechos Civiles, UCLA, January 2010), http://escholarship.org/uc/item/4r07q8kg.

4. Ibid.

5. In Pauline Lipman, *High Stakes Education: Inequality, Globalization, and Urban School Reform* (New York: Routledge, 2011).

6. "Get the Facts About Charter Schools in Illinois," Illinois Network of Charter Schools, https://www.incschools.org/about-charters/get-the -facts, accessed March 30, 2017.

7. "Charter School Directory," New York City Department of Education, http://schools.nyc.gov/community/charters/information /directory.htm.

8. S. Mann, "Slavery, Sharecropping, and Sexual Inequality," *Signs* 14, no. 4 (1989): 774–98.

9. Chicago International Charter School website, last modified 2017, http://www.chicagointl.org/about/careers.html.

10. Michelle Fine and Michael Fabricant, *Charter Schools and the Corporate Makeover of Public Education: What's at Stake?* (New York: Teachers College, 2012), 63.

11. Pauline Lipman, "Chicago School Policy: Regulating Black and Latino Youth in the Global City," *Race Ethnicity and Education* 6, no. 4 (2003): 331–55; Lipman, *High Stakes Education*; Pauline Lipman, *The New Political Economy of Urban Education: Neoliberalism, Race, and the Right to the City* (New York: Routledge, 2011); Kenneth Saltman, *Capitalizing on Disaster: Taking and Breaking Public Schools* (New York: Routledge, 2007); Kenneth Saltman, *The Failure of Corporate School Reform* (New York: Routledge, 2012).

12. Heather Cherone, "War of Words Escalates Between Claypool and Rauner over CPS Budget Crisis," *DNA Info*, February 8, 2017, https:// www.dnainfo.com/chicago/20170208/wrigleyville/war-of-words -escalates-between-claypool-rauner-over-cps-budget-crisis.

13. Civic Committee of the Commercial Club of Chicago, *Left Behind: Student Achievement in Chicago's Public Schools* (Chicago: The Committee, 2003).

14. Ibid.

15. "About AUSL," Academy for Urban School Leadership, http://auslchicago.org/about.

16. Dan Mihalopoulos, "Former UNO Boss Juan Rangel Broke Securities Law, SEC Says," *Chicago Sun-Times*, June 25, 2016, http://chicago.suntimes.com/news/former-uno-boss-juan-rangel-broke-securities-law-sec-says/.

17. "Charter School Collecting Steep Disciplinary Fines from Low-Income Families: Report," *Huffington Post*, February 16, 2012, http://www.huffingtonpost.com/2012/02/14/noble-street-charter-scho_n_1276100.html.

18. Illinois News Network, "Chicago Set to Become First U.S. City to Cap Charter-School Growth with Union Contract," October 12, 2016, https://ilnews.org/10395/chicago-set-to-become-first-u-s-city-to-cap-charter-school-growth-with-union-contract.

19. Valerie Strauss, "NAACP Moves Ahead with Its Call for Moratorium on Charter Schools," *Washington Post*, December 6, 2016, https://www.washingtonpost.com/news/answer-sheet/wp/2016/12/06/naacp-moves-ahead-with-its-call-for-moratorium-on-charter-schools/?utm_term=.d929e7e73417.

20. Carol Caref, Justin Hilgendorf, Pavlyn Jankov, Sarah Hainds, and Jordan Conwell, "A Just Chicago: Fighting for the City Our Students Deserve," Chicago Teachers Union, February 2015, http://ajustchicago.org/wp-content/uploads/2015/06/A_Just_Chicago.pdf.

NEW YORK CITY—TERRENDA WHITE: *From Community Schools to Charter Chains*

1. Michael Walrond Jr., "Roots for Revolutionaries, Part I" (sermon), July 28, 2013, First Corinthian Baptist Church media library, http://www.fcbcnyc.org/media-library. Walrond (aka Pastor Mike) is a community organizer and senior minister at First Corinthian Baptist Church in Harlem, New York City. He ran (unsuccessfully) in the 2014 Democratic primary in the Thirteenth Congressional District of New York.

2. Author's field notes, October 2011.

3. Author's field notes, June 2012.

4. Author's field notes, August 2013.

5. Albert Shanker, "National Press Club Speech," March 31, 1988, http://reuther.wayne.edu/files/64.43.pdf; Richard Kahlenberg and Halley Potter, *A Smarter Charter: Finding What Works for Charter Schools and Public Education* (New York: Teachers College Press, 2014).

6. New York City Charter School Center, *Charter School Facts 2012–13* (New York City: NY Department of Education, 2012), http://www.nyccharterschools.org/sites/default/files/resources/charter_school

_facts_082912.pdf; New York City Independent Budget Office, *School Indicators for New York City Charter Schools, 2013–2014 School Year* (New York: July 2015), http://www.ibo.nyc.ny.us/iboreports/school -indicators-for-new-york-city-charter-schools-2013-2014-school-year -july-2015.pdf.

7. John Kucsera and Gary Orfield, *New York State's Extreme School Segregation: Inequality, Inaction, and a Damaged Future* (Los Angeles: Civil Rights Project/Proyecto Derechos Civiles, 2014), https://civil-rightsproject.ucla.edu/research/k-12-education/integration-and -diversity/ny-norflet-re- port-placeholder/Kucsera-New-York -Extreme-Segregation-2014.pdf.

8. Jerald E. Podair, *The Strike That Changed New York: Blacks, Whites, and the Ocean Hill-Brownsville Crisis* (New Haven, CT: Yale University Press, 2002); Heather Lewis, *New York Public Schools: From Brownsville to Bloomberg; Community Control and Its Legacy* (New York: Teachers College Press, 2013); Charles E. Wilson, "Education in Harlem—I.S. 201 in Perspective," in *Harlem U.S.A.*, ed. John Henrik Clarke (New York: Collier Macmillan, 1971).

9. Podair, *The Strike That Changed New York*; Lewis, *New York Public Schools*; Lisa M. Stulberg, *Race, Schools, and Hope: African Americans and School Choice After Brown* (New York: Teachers College Press, 2008). Indeed, a lawsuit against the State of New York (Campaign for Fiscal Equity v. State of New York, 100 N.Y. 2d 893, 908 [NY 2003]), led by Michael Rebell and the Campaign for Fiscal Equity, resulted in a ruling by a court of appeals, in *Campaign for Fiscal Equity v. State of New York*, declaring that the constitutional right of New York City's children to a "sound basic education" was violated, warranting additional funds totaling between $5 billion and $9 billion. See Campaign for Educational Equity, *Students' Constitutional Right to a Sound Basic Education: New York State's Unfinished Agenda*, http://www.equitycampaign.org/publications/safeguard-ing-students-educational-rights/NY's-Unfinished-Agenda-Part-I. -Roadmap-Final-(11-25-16).pdf.

10. New York State Charter Schools Act, 1998. Education Law, §§ 2850–2857.

11. Amber Charter School, "Who Are We," May 2, 2017, http://www .ambercharter.org/Page/28.

12. SUNY Charter Schools Institute, *Harbor Science Charter School: Evaluation Report, 2001–2002* (New York: Charter Schools Institute, 2002), http://www.newyorkcharters.org/wp-content/uploads/Harbor -Science-and-Arts-School-Evaluation-2001-02.pdf.

13. SUNY Charter Schools Institute, "Sisulu-Walker Charter School: School Opens," http://www.newyorkcharters.org/progress/schools /sisulu-walker-charter-school.

14. SUNY Charter Schools Institute, "Renewal Recommendation Report: Sisulu-Walker Charter School of Harlem," http://www.newyork charters.org/wp-content/uploads/A7_Sisulu-Walker-2015-16-Renewal -Recommendation-Report-FINAL.pdf.

15. Gary Miron and Charisse Gulosimo define an education management organization (EMO) as "a private organization or firm that manages public schools, including district and charter public schools," in *Profiles of For-Profit and Nonprofit Education Management Organizations, Fourteenth Edition—2011–2012* (Boulder, CO: National Education Policy Center, 2013), http://nepc.colorado.edu/publication/EMO-profiles-11-12.

16. After 2010, new charter schools in New York were no longer allowed the option of contracting with for-profit organizations. As such, only a dozen existing schools contracted with a for-profit EMO in 2010.

17. New York City Independent Budget Office, *School Indicators for New York City Charter Schools, 2013–2014 School Year; The State of the Charter Sector* (New York: New York City Department of Education, 2012), http://www.nyccharterschools.org/sites/default/files/resources /state-of-the-sector-2012.pdf.

18. C. Farrell, P. Wohlstetter, and J. Smith, "Charter Management Organizations: An Emerging Approach to Scaling Up What Works," *Educational Policy* 26, no. 4 (2012): 499–532.

19. Gary Miron and Jessica L. Urschel, *Profiles of Nonprofit Education Management Organizations: 2009–2010* (Boulder, CO: National Education Policy Center, 2010), http://nepc.colorado.edu/publication /EMO-NP-09–10; Janelle Scott and Catherine C. DiMartino, "Hybridized, Franchised, Duplicated, and Replicated: Charter Schools and Management Organizations," in *The Charter School Experiment: Expectations, Evidence, and Implications*, ed. Christopher Lubienski and Peter C. Weitzel (Cambridge, MA: Harvard Education Press, 2010).

20. Jennifer Jennings, "School Choice or Schools' Choice? Managing in an Era of Accountability," *Sociology of Education* 83 (2010): 227–47.

21. My count of charter schools in Harlem is drawn from school websites and the New York City Department of Education *Directory of New York City Charter Schools 2013–2014* (New York: New York City Department of Education, 2014), http://schools.nyc.gov/NR/rdonlyres /8E63FBF3-1106-4AD2-A52F-1FEBDB243B13/0/CSDirectory1314 _Introduction.pdf. Counts varied each year, however, between 2012–2013 and 2013–2014 (the duration of study), and ranged from forty-two to forty-four charter schools, due to new charter schools opening, existing charter schools closing, and charter relocations to other boroughs.

22. New York City Independent Budget Office, *School Indicators for New York City Charter Schools, 2013–2014 School Year.*

23. While there were approximately fifty-nine charter schools in Manhattan in 2012, nearly three-quarters (forty-four) were located in the Harlem neighborhood. For example, of Manhattan's six community school districts (CSDs), those in Harlem had the highest number of charter schools, with CSD 5 (Central Harlem) having the most (approximately twenty-two). CSD 4 (East Harlem) had approximately eleven and CSD 3 (the Upper West Side and Harlem) had approximately twelve.

24. New York City Charter School Center, *The State of the NYC Charter School Sector* (New York: New York City Charter School Center, 2012), http://www.nyccharterschools.org/sites/default/files/resources/state-of-the-sector-2012.pdf.

25. Kucsera and Orfield, *New York State's Extreme School Segregation*.

26. Kristen Buras, Jim Randels, Kalamu ya Salaam, and Students at the Center, *Pedagogy, Policy, and the Privatized City: Stories of Dispossession and Defiance from New Orleans* (New York: Teachers College Press, 2010); Pauline Lipman, *The New Political Economy of Urban Education: Neoliberalism, Race, and the Right to the City* (New York: Routledge, 2004); Rhody A. McCoy, "The Formation of a Community-Controlled School District," in *Community Control of Schools*, ed. Henry Levin (Washington, DC: Brookings Institution, 1970), 169–89.

27. Bruce Baker, *Exploring the Consequences of Charter School Expansion in US Cities* (Washington, DC: Economic Policy Institute, November, 2016); E. Frankenberg and C. Lee, "Charter Schools and Race: A Lost Opportunity for Integrated Education," *Education Policy Analysis Archives* 11, no. 32 (2003), http://epaa.asu.edu/ojs/article/view/260.

28. J. Golann, "The Paradox of Success at a No-Excuses School," *Sociology of Education* 88, no. 2 (2015): 103–19; Jenn Hatfield and Michael Q. McShane, *Measuring Diversity in Charter School Offerings* (Washington, DC: American Enterprise Institute, July 2015), http://www.aei.org/wp- content/uploads/2015/07/Measuring-Diversity-in-Charter-School-Offerings.pdf; Abigail Thernstrom and Stephan Thernstrom, *No Excuses: Closing the Racial Gap in Learning* (New York: Simon and Schuster, 2003); Terrenda White, "Charter Schools: Demystifying Whiteness in a Market of 'No Excuses' Corporate-Styled Charter Schools," in *What's Race Got to Do With It? How Current School Reform Policy Maintains Racial and Economic Inequality*, ed. Bree Picower and Edwin Mayorga (New York: Peter Lang, 2015).

29. New York City Charter School Center, *The State of the NYC Charter School Sector*.

30. One exception is the Sisulu-Walker Charter School of Harlem, which maintained its stand-alone status while contracting with an EMO for vendor services related to payroll, accounting, and human resources.

31. In some states, CMOs/EMOs are actual "charter holders" governing schools. In contrast, New York's charter law stipulates that the holder of a charter is a school's board of trustees, which governs the school. As such, boards of trustees (charter holders) can enter into agreements with CMOs for the operation and management of schools.

32. Author interview, September 12, 2012.

33. New York State Charter Schools Act, 1998.

34. Ibid.

35. Author interview, July 22, 2013.

36. Author interview, July 22, 2013.

37. Author interview, July 22, 2013.

38. Author interview, August 14, 2013.

39. Gary Miron, Jessica L. Urschel, and Nicholas Saxton, *What Makes KIPP Work? A Study of Student Characteristics, Attrition, and School Finance* (New York: National Center for the Study of Privatization in Education, Teachers College, Columbia University/ Study Group on Educational Management Organizations at Western Michigan University, 2011), http://www.edweek.org/media/kippstudy.pdf.

40. Author interview, July 26, 2013.

41. Author interview, July 26, 2013.

42. Author interview, January 10, 2013.

43. Author interview, January 10, 2013.

44. Author interview, January 10, 2013.

45. Author interview, December 19, 2012.

46. Author interview, December 19, 2012.

47. Author interview, December 19, 2012.

48. Author interview, September 12, 2012.

49. Author interview, February 2, 2013.

50. Author interview, July 26, 2013.

51. Author interview, January 10, 2013.

52. Author interview, January 10, 2013.

53. Author interview, January 9, 2013.

54. Author interview, December 17, 2012.

55. Author interview, December 17, 2012.

56. Author interview, August 21, 2013.

57. Author interview, September 6, 2012.

58. Author interview, December 17, 2012.

59. Author interview, December 17, 2012.

60. Author interview, December 17, 2012.

61. Author interview, September 12, 2012.

62. Author interview, January 10, 2013.

63. Author interview, January 10, 2013.

64. This concept is rooted in critical race theory and seeks to shift "the research lens away from a deficit view of Communities of Color as places full of cultural poverty disadvantages, and instead focuses on and learns from the array of cultural knowledge, skills, abilities and contacts possessed by socially marginalized groups that often go unrecognized and unacknowledged," in T. J. Yosso, "Whose Culture Has Capital? A Critical Race Theory Discussion of Community Cultural Wealth," *Race Ethnicity and Education* 8, no. 1 (2005): 69.